EVOLVING

PRACTICAL
STRATEGIES FOR
UNLEASHING YOUR
TRUE LEADERSHIP
POTENTIAL

DR. MABLE A. ALFRED

Copyright © 2024 Dr. Mable A. Alfred
All rights reserved.

No part of this publication may be reproduced, distributed, or transmitted in any form or by any means, including photocopying, recording, or other electronic or mechanical methods, without th e prior written permission of the author, except in the case of brief quotations embodied in critical reviews and certain other noncommercial uses permitted by copyright law. For permission requests, contact the author at the email below.

Evolving
Practical Strategies for Unleashing Your True Leadership Potential

Dr. Mable A. Alfred
Drmalfred@yahoo.com

ISBN 978-1-943342-33-4

Printed in the United States of America
Destined To Publish
www.destinedtopublish.com

To my loving parents, Samuel and Gloria Harston. I am all that I am because of your love and support.

ACKNOWLEDGMENTS

I'd like to acknowledge my three amazing heartbeats: Gloria, Dawnielle, and Liana. My love and commitment to them have served as my most powerful motivators, inspiring me to excel in every endeavor.

CONTENTS

Leadership: The Evolution

Chapter 1 – Leadership: The Evolution — 1
Reaching the Top — 4
The Cycle of Leadership — 8

The Honeymoon

Chapter 2 – Humble Beginnings — 15
BOLD Moves — 17
READY for Leadership — 18
Liker-Ship — 20
Principles of KNOWING — 21
The Journey — 31
Cruise Ship vs. Battleship — 32
The Journey — 34

Chapter 3 – Gaining Momentum: Power — 36
Starting Power — 36
Staying Power — 37
Wonder-Working Power — 40
MO Power — 41
MO Better Blues – Finding the Pulse — 44

Establishing Purpose

Chapter 4 – Lead Out Loud – Living Your Purpose — 47
Finding and Sustaining Your Purpose — 47
Drafting My Own Narratives — 51
Leadership Pledges — 53

From Pledge to Progress	54
Becoming an A-Lister	55

Gaining Insight

Chapter 5 – Insightful Leadership — 61
- Gaining Insight — 62
- Epiphanies — 65
- Foresight — 66
- Hindsight — 66
- Sight Unseen — 67

Distractions

Chapter 6 – The Many Shades of Darkness — 71
- Leadership in Despair — 72
- Regrouping, Rearranging, and Reflecting Through Darkness — 73
- What the Heavens – When the Agendas Don't Match — 77
- Quiet to Chaos or Chaos to Quiet — 78
- Shades of Darkness – Taking Steps of Faith through Darkness — 80
- When Darkness Comes — 82
- Weathering the Storms – Learning to Dance in the Rain — 84

Chapter 7 – Break Every Chain — 85
- Invisible Chains — 88
- Breakthrough — 89
- Leadership Breakthrough — 90
- Breakdowns — 92
- The "Be" Attitudes of Leadership — 94
- Breakthrough! — 96

Chapter 8 – If the Truth Hurts — 98
- Guard Your Truth — 99
- The Truth Shall Set You Free — 104

Survival

Chapter 9 – A Hill to Die On ... 109
- Prevention Is Key ... 113
- Restoring Leadership ... 115
- No Time to Die ... 117

Chapter 10 – Fit to Be Tied ... 119
- Survival of the Fittest ... 119
- I Choose Survival ... 124
- Be in the Know ... 126

Leader-Shift

Chapter 11 – Consider the Shift – Don't Stay Too Long ... 131
- In Pursuit of Sanity ... 135
- When the Writing Is on the Wall ... 140
- History vs. Destiny ... 142
- Changing the Game ... 143
- After This ... 147

References ... 151

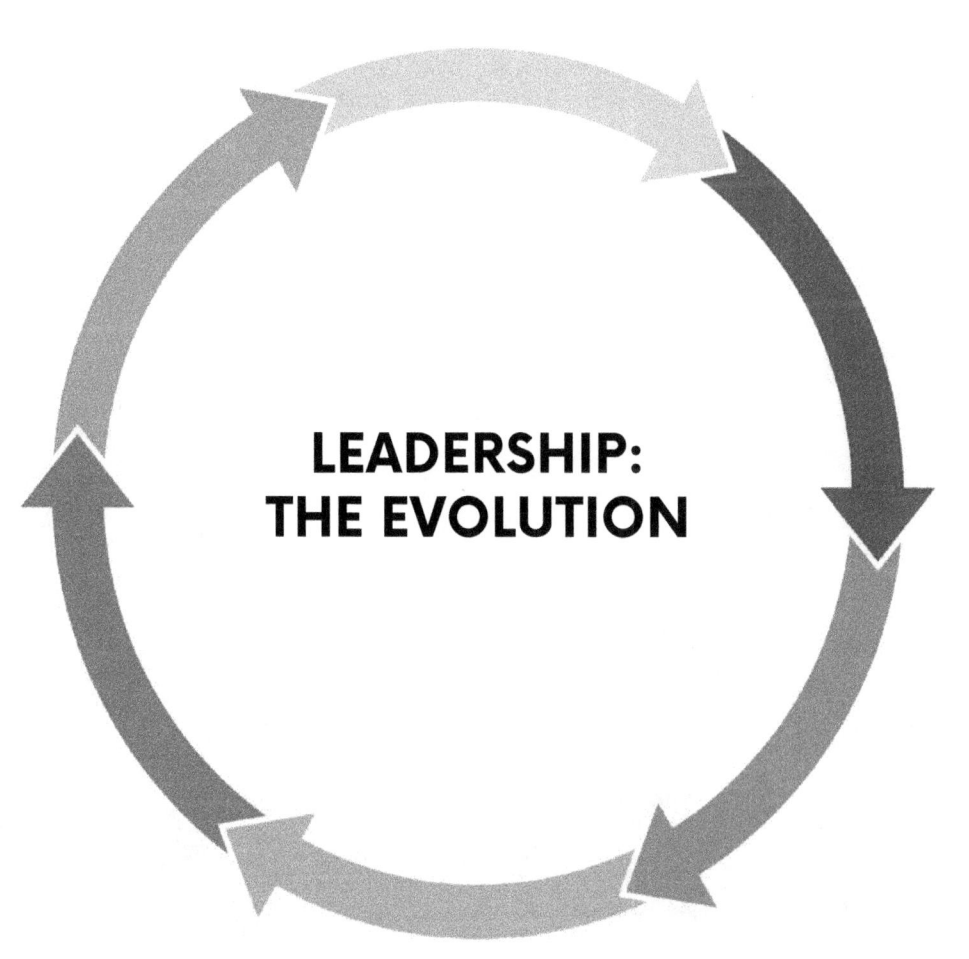

LEADERSHIP: THE EVOLUTION

CHAPTER 1

LEADERSHIP: THE EVOLUTION

"Greatness is not a function of circumstance. Greatness, it turns out, is largely a matter of conscious choice, and discipline." —
Jim Collins, Good to Great

In today's world, leadership is an evolution. Leaders aren't simply made; they continually evolve. It's not a swift process or an occurrence through osmosis but a gradual refinement of a perpetually changing skill set. Leadership takes time and work. Regardless of the field or industry, leaders invariably seek strategies for transformation, traditionally exploring avenues to achieve bigger and better outcomes within their organizations.

Leadership has been around since the beginning of time. It is complicated, but selecting the right path to travel is paramount. Leaders are a dime a dozen. You are not the first leader, and you will not be the last. Some leaders are made, and some are born. The true test is how you distinguish yourself from others on this journey. No matter what kind of leader you are or seek to be, you must live out the purpose of your leadership. Why do you want to lead, and what makes you a great leader? What is your ultimate goal as a result of your leadership? What is your WHY?

Leadership is an imperfect situation. There is no such thing as the perfect leadership role. It inevitably comes with successes and challenges. However, one can take an imperfect leadership situation and make it work. These situations can make you bitter—or they can make you better. Being armed with the right strategies can change the trajectory of your leadership.

Striving for perfection in leadership is misguided and can lead to epic failure. Leadership is an ever-evolving situation and will never be perfect, but it can be fruitful. And while it can be fruitful, it can also be frustrating. There are many books and articles about effective leadership. Maybe you've attended numerous conferences and classes to make you a great leader in your respective field. However, implementing or even recalling those strategies afterward can often prove elusive or ineffective.

Evolution means to change over time. This entails growth and development in all aspects. You should never leave a leadership role in the same form as when you entered. The beginning of the leadership process is where the leader formulates, defines, and learns about their new environment. They formulate what type of leader they are; they define how they will use their leadership type to navigate through their role; and they learn how their respective style fits into the system they are leading.

You must be ready for leadership. Not everyone seeking such a role is necessarily ready for it, and it's perfectly okay to decide you are not ready. Before accepting the role, you must know who you are as a leader. Are you an annual or a perennial leader? Will your leadership die off at the end of a season, or will it last? Imagine planting a seed that will soon turn into a beautiful flower. It must first be watered and cultivated before it can take root downward for the beauty to show upward. A seed produces roots that grow down and become strongly planted in the foundation of the earth. Only through the power of strong roots can a plant grow. Strong roots require nurturing. In the same way, great leaders that last must be strongly planted in all aspects of their work.

An evolution is like a movement. Movements are temporary events that lead to permanent change and lifelong actions. Likewise, leadership is temporary, but it's up to the leader to make it an ongoing, permanent action. A movement brings people together for a common purpose and has an end goal. It has leaders who connect with people to buy into the vision and mission of the cause, but the movement ultimately reaches far beyond its leader and its people. Leadership can be a series of movements with many steps, cycles, and phases. Just continue to allow those steps, however large or small, to evolve. The smallest step could set off the largest impact. But you must look for and be prepared for those land mines that will curtail or halt your progress. You must use your power wisely and effectively if you want to come out on top.

No area of leadership is at a standstill, and you are not going to be prepared for half of what you encounter, so you must be resolute in your words and actions. Even though you won't be prepared for everything, you must get ready and stay ready for anything. Getting ready is knowing—and having—what is required in great leadership. You must be ready for the unexpected and the unknown, including distractions that will take your attention away from your goal. Otherwise, these distractions could ultimately keep you from progressing as a leader and shorten your leadership journey.

Land mines will be unavoidable. Be prepared, because you will inevitably step on some of them along your journey. Navigate through the turmoil of the land mines, but quickly move forward, only looking back to admire and learn from your challenges and successes. As leaders, we have the ultimate power to overcome these land mines by being equipped with the necessary strategies to surmount the barriers that will hold us back. These barriers may come at any stage of the journey. Leadership comes with many moving parts, and perfection is not the goal; survival is the goal. Knowing the cycles of leadership helps you overcome the barriers that lie within each cycle, and it's a recipe for a successful and fulfilling leadership journey. Understanding the cycles allows leaders to press forward.

Reaching the Top

> Leadership in any capacity can be lonely. As a matter of fact, life at the top gets even more lonely as storms form and trouble elevates, because your colleagues and peers are busy leading their own organizations. The darkest days of my 35-year career were the years spent in leadership roles, yet those years were the most rewarding.
>
> Nothing—absolutely nothing—about leadership is easy. I'd like to share my unadulterated experiences of being a leader, with all the lessons learned and wisdom acquired.
>
> My first role as a leader was being a teacher leader. It was a small role that showed me that leadership was in my future, although I was only a leader when there was a need to lead my grade level team.
>
> Much later, after more than 20 years engaged in various leadership roles, I thought I had arrived when I reached the CEO seat. I had been relatively successful in all of my lower leadership roles, which is how I ended up in the top

seat. I truly felt this was it for me. This was the seat I had always dreamed about. This was the seat all leaders in my field strived for. This was it—or so I thought.

When I reached the top leadership seat, I was unaware of the many land mines. I had always looked at the position from the outside in, so I was unaware of how it operated from the inside out. Due to my lack of knowledge, early on in my tenure, a few land mines blew up in my face. It took years to recover from these extreme blowups.

I would encourage the following for anyone who is aspiring to leadership:

- Research the job from the inside out—know what you are getting into.
- Examine your life before accepting the job—stay knowledgeable.
- Get and maintain a spiritual connection—stay humble.
- Be at peace with a total life change—stay flexible.
- Be prepared for anything and everything—stay persistent.

I thought I knew what my leadership would be like based on my past practices. I was wrong. This experience was not just a new chapter, but a new book with multiple chapters—a book that I not only hadn't ever read but didn't even know existed. I realized for the first time in my career that I was leading with blinders on, and actually, it wasn't at all how I thought it would be.

I thought I was ready. I had done my homework. I did extensive research and created a plan of action to be implemented. I had years of experience at every level, and I was a master in the field. I did everything my training courses taught me to do. I knew I was ready! Yet I reached a brick wall before

I even got to my one-year tenure mark. This was initially a devastating experience.

I was too confident. I did not just feel I was a gifted leader; others had told me so. I went into this position knowing I was gifted to thrive. But reality informed me that there is a price to pay for true success, and I was about to pay it.

What I had not anticipated was that leadership looks and feels different at each level. My other experiences of leadership had been different, and I thought I could carry over some of the same leadership styles. I was armed—but with the wrong weapons. I was armed with the wrong knowledge needed to be successful in my new role at the top. Unfortunately, this led me down a dangerous path.

This became the most challenging period of all my leadership experiences. Because of my success in my previous roles, I thought I was unstoppable. I thought I could do the same things I had always done and success would follow me. My leadership ability went from light to darkness instantly. My entire world seemed to shatter, and I had no direction.

I went into the position ignorant of the culture and climate of the organization. I walked into the unknown at the hands of a school board with their own agendas and aspirations. I had been involved in workplace politics, but here, the political climate was so thick one could cut it with a knife. I had never known politics at this level ... and the politics were not even focused on the core and mission of the organization.

I began to have self-doubt about my ability as a leader. My belief in my knowledge, ability, and past experiences hit an all-time low. I was beaten down by the board, the unions, the staff, outside interest groups, and the community. I became traumatized by the hatred, agendas, harassment, negativity, and lack of true governance. My initial thought was to run and never look back. But I was stuck because I was nearly 30 years vested in this field and bound by a contract. More importantly, I was invested in my leadership and my purpose for leading. I had to be a victor, not a victim. I knew I had to reclaim and rely on my lifelong purpose and my WHY.

I had to get beyond the message that the elected board was conveying: that my humanity was worthless. I had to get beyond the other stakeholders pulling at me from different directions. I had to gather what little dignity I could muster and create my own humanity despite the problems, chaos, and dysfunction I had signed on to. I had to realize that I had not gotten to this point in my career to lose sight of my humanity or my WHY. I had to acknowledge that through my humanity, I carry an inestimable worth. I had to realize that my human nature was not the problem. I also had to realize that I had spent nearly all of my life in a field I loved because I wanted to make a difference for others. Lastly, I had to realize the problem was not me but external factors of a long, deep-rooted governing culture that I happened to inherit.

I was not broken! A system was broken, and I happened to be selected to lead it. This organization was bleeding culturally, and I could either be helpless or hopeful despite the actions of the governing board. The actions of the board manifested themselves in everything I encountered, and I had to stop the bleeding.

All emergencies require intercession. I first had to forget all the knowledge I had acquired over many years and place myself under the authority of an uneducated, uninformed board for the first time in my career—those whose thinking was in the political realm and who came with personal and very aggressive agendas. Faulty governance began impeding my leadership early in my tenure. I searched for answers in books and classes, but they were not helpful.

I had acquired physical, mental, and emotional insecurities about my leadership—insecurities I had never experienced in my three-decade career. I soon learned that I had to manage my insecurities about my new world in the top leadership seat. I had to shift those mental insecurities to a world of composed certainty. This was not an overnight process but a process that had to evolve. In fact, it took several years of trauma before I gained peace and really understood how to navigate my role in the top position.

My leadership went through several phases within a cycle that enabled me to grow and develop. From my experiences, I determined that there are six phases of leadership. Navigating through and understanding this cycle of six phases helped me to evolve in leadership and be successful in the top seat. The six phases of the cycle are Honeymoon, Establishing Purpose, Gaining Insight, Distractions, Survival, and Leader-Shift.

I will expound on each area of the cycle from my leadership perspective.

The Cycle of Leadership

Beginning a new leadership journey is like merging boats that are going in different directions into one ship heading in one direction. The cycle illustrated below will assist you in your journey through leadership, whether you're a new or tenured leader. This cycle shows that leadership is an inward experience that must be cultivated outwardly, an understanding that will prepare you for growth and development in your role at the top. If you're a new leader, this illustration will help you get your feet grounded from the beginning and become rooted in your work. If you're a more tenured leader, you will find that the cycle will nurture you in weakened areas of your journey and will help you take charge of your personal growth as a leader.

THE CYCLE

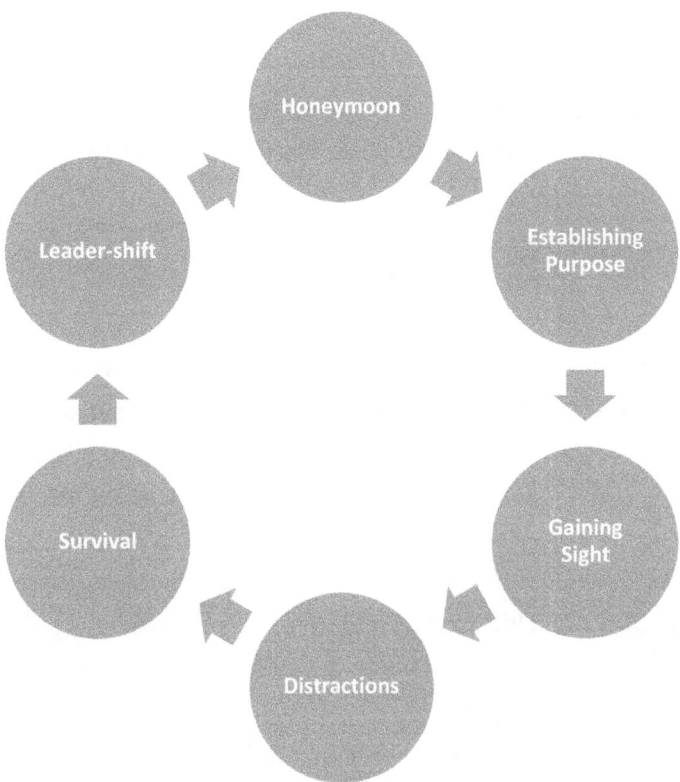

As the illustration above shows, leadership is a cycle that evolves. This cycle describes the progression of phases I traveled through during my leadership journey—a progression any leadership journey could travel. As I began to be aware of the journey, it became easier to manipulate each phase.

A leader can travel through each phase in sequential order but may also skip one or more phases; this cycle is cyclical but can be recursive. It is never ending; it can repeat any phase at any time. A leader may travel from the Honeymoon phase and, depending on circumstances, jump to the Leader-Shift phase and leave just as quickly as they entered. A leader may also go through Establishing Purpose and Gaining Insight simultaneously.

Every leader is different, and you may travel your own unique path for success in leadership. However, all leaders need to know how to survive when their leadership hits a challenging phase. The following chapters will show you how to recognize the challenges and be equipped with the proper tools to keep your leadership on track and moving toward success.

The chapters of this book will enable you to prepare for the challenges, seen and unseen, that you will face as a leader. To grow, evolve, and achieve sustainability, leaders must know how to identify and react to these challenges and have the tools and strategies to navigate their leadership experience.

THE PHASES OF THE LEADERSHIP CYCLE ARE:

HONEYMOON
The honeymoon is where leaders are adjusting to their new seat. Everything is usually quiet because the new leader is adapting to the organization. The honeymoon is where you determine what type of leader you are and how you will use that leadership style to drive organizational success. It is a time that demands your undivided attention.

ESTABLISHING PURPOSE

Leaders must know and be able to articulate what they want to accomplish and why they want to accomplish it. Every leader must have a purpose for what they do. This phase is where their leadership begins to develop a vision, a mission, and goals to drive the leadership. The leader is thinking about the impact they will have on the organization.

GAINING INSIGHT

This phase is when the leader learns to listen to their intuition. It tests the leader's ability to ignite understanding and awareness, with the end result being the expansion of their leadership reach.

DISTRACTIONS

A leader will encounter inevitable distractions on the path to success. However, a good leader approaches every obstacle as a learning experience. During this phase, a leader develops the tools necessary to overcome any distraction. This section of the book identifies some of the distractions leaders will incur and offers interesting tools to help overcome them.

SURVIVAL

In addition to small distractions, leaders will also encounter catastrophic storms. With an understanding of this phase, leaders will be better equipped to survive the storms that will inevitably form. Survival can be tough for all types of leaders. The goal is to survive through this cycle and avoid having to make any unwanted shifts. The chapters relative to this phase offer tools to weather any storm that might hinder your leadership.

LEADER-SHIFT

Leader-shift means changing course. This can involve departing the role but staying in the game, or even leaving the profession altogether. When it's time to go, it's time to go. This concluding chapter alerts leaders to the messages that will signal the end of their leadership run and will help them develop an exit or reform strategy.

One aspect of successful leadership is the ability to learn the phases of the cycle you are traveling through, understand what strategies you will need to navigate through the phases, and effectively use the strategies to garner success.

Whether you are a fresh or tenured leader, analyzing these phases will help you transform your practices in order to navigate any situation. And no matter what phase you find yourself in, a leader must always be evolving.

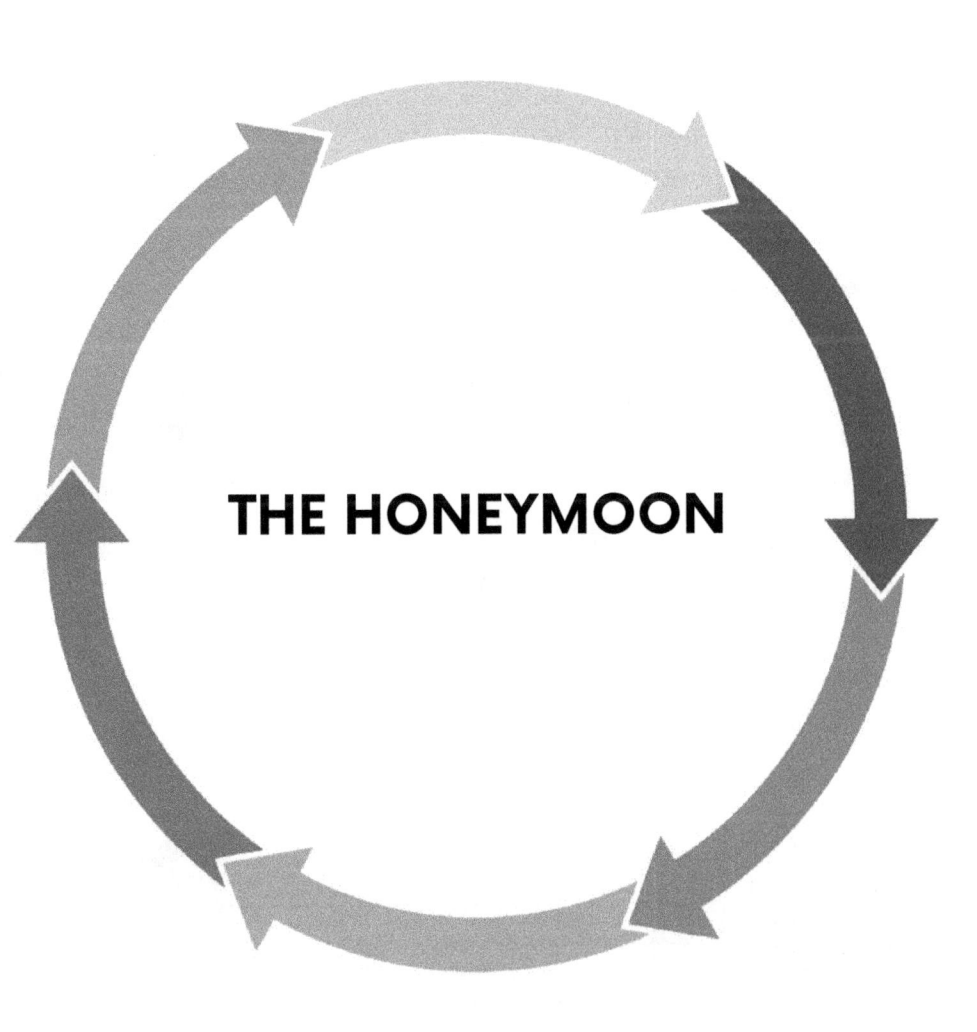

CHAPTER 2

HUMBLE BEGINNINGS

"The beginning is the most important part of the work." —Plato
"Watch what they do, observe how they do it, and examine what makes them feel content." —Confucius

A "honeymoon period" is the initial stage of the leadership journey. Whether you are new to the role or a veteran, this is where the leadership cycle begins. It is a period of grace and special leniency enjoyed by a first-time leader, but it is a temporary stage that should be approached as a springboard for growth. It's an important first phase of work; it is a time when the new leader sets the stage for their leadership, identifies key players, examines the culture, learns more about the work, and builds relationships with their governing board. It is also during this stage that the leader gets to know their staff and their board, sets ground rules, seeks approval, identifies challenges, and develops goals.

A honeymoon can last from two months to two years and can be marked by lots of reform, rearranging, reflection, and replacements. A leader must understand the key elements that will extend or shorten the honeymoon period. This is the important first phase of the leadership experience, and this period of new beginnings should set the stage for the rest of the leadership journey.

New leaders do not always understand the context and the challenges of being at the top. They must gain knowledge during this phase in order to be successful during the subsequent phases. Extending the length of the honeymoon phase can be crucial to the existence of the leader. However, a short honeymoon does not have to be synonymous with a short tenure. It can simply mean you have to be equipped and move intentionally throughout your leadership.

Most new leaders enter their position with great optimism based on their past practices and confidence in what they know they bring to the role. New leaders enjoy this period because of its novelty and freshness. The honeymoon period is marked by acceptance and a lack of stress, and you are usually working for the same person, board, or trustees who hired you and who have faith in your capability to do the job. They know you from your resume, interview, references, statements, and other information collected during the hiring process.

Many times, when a top leader's hiring is at the hands of a political or elected board, a honeymoon period can be cut short by the next election. Typically, in political races, the candidate runs with an agenda to undo everything the incumbent has put into place ... including the seating of the top leader. Their first order of business after taking the oath of office is to push their agenda forward. Whether a board of trustees, education directors, or governors, these are the groups that oversee an organization. Top leaders must learn to adapt and must have the ability and tools to navigate these structures successfully.

Usually, if the leader is hired by a structured board, that honeymoon period lasts as long as that board exists. It is this group of stakeholders that directed the human resources department to develop the job description, seek a hiring firm, review resumes, interview candidates, and determine which candidate was the best fit for the top seat.

Leaders begin by setting the tone for the culture and atmosphere of the organization with which they have been entrusted. One can create a positive atmosphere or a negative atmosphere. It is essential to know where people fit into that atmosphere so that you can arrange it accordingly.

Leaders must be willing to make courageous and bold moves. These moves will often be unpopular, uncomfortable, and unapologetic. Such decisions will move the needle of change but grow your leadership. As such, these moves will help the organization to grow and prosper as well.

BOLD Moves

The honeymoon phase can make or break one's leadership experience, so it must be carefully navigated. It can set the tone and the needs for the leadership journey. To navigate the honeymoon period, a new leader's entrance must be **BOLD** and courageous.

Going into leadership is a BOLD move. It takes a BOLD person to become a leader and begin a leadership journey. One must enter with the thoughts of being **B**rave enough to **O**versee **L**asting **D**eliverables. Leadership is not for the faint of heart. It takes **B**uilding **O**utstanding and **L**ofty **D**epartments. It takes **B**alancing an **O**rganization with **L**oyalty and **D**iscipline. As you begin your leadership, you have great work to accomplish. Unfortunately, there is no such thing as perfect leadership. Perfection in leadership is housed only in our minds, not in reality. Therefore, you must enter with the **B**elief and **O**ptimism that your leadership will be **L**asting and **D**riven by success.

New leaders must adapt to new conditions and outlooks. Accept your truth about who you are and about whether you are ready for this new evolutionary moment in your life—a moment that will bring new experiences:

- new routines
- new thoughts
- new focus
- new goals
- new missions
- new actions
- new mindsets

You must evolve as a leader in order to keep up with the organization, which is also evolving around you. Everything in life changes. Nothing remains the same, not even leadership.

READY for Leadership

To enjoy a sustainable leadership, a leader must be open to the evolution process from the beginning, evolving through the many phases of the leadership cycle and surviving at all costs. This means you will have ups and downs, but you must be resilient throughout.

The leadership career you take on must be the right fit for you. Beginning leadership can have a short or long season. Do not expect a long season when you are only approaching it with a short-season mentality—giving short-term expectations, exhibiting a short commitment, or planning for a short time.

Leadership is a unique journey that one must be prepared for. When taking on a leadership role and expecting a long season, you prepare for the season. When the time comes, you have to BE READY. You must agree to do the following:

- **BE READY** to step into some big shoes. If the shoes do not fit, be ready to try a new pair … or consider trying on some boots. You'll need the right mindset and the right skill set, just as you need the proper footwear for different occasions.
- **GET READY** for the good, the bad, and sometimes the ugly. Getting ready can entail setting goals, planning, and determining what success does and doesn't look like.
- **STAY READY** for anything that may come your way. Staying ready takes tenacity and resilience to keep forging ahead for the good of the organization.

Beginning leadership is not an easy feat. Before embarking on the role, study the atmosphere and pre-existing culture. Determine if you are willing to merge your goals with an existing culture and atmosphere to create a new beat.

Sitting in the top seat may seem like a glamorous role, but what you perceive from the outside is totally different from what really goes on behind the scenes. Leadership is not for the faint of heart.

Leadership can be the fight of your life—especially if it does not begin well. Sometimes it takes daily fighting to garner respect that will lead to success. You will find yourself fighting staff, unions, and boards, as well as other constituents.

Liker-Ship

Being liked as a leader is naturally desirable, but it's only part of the equation. True leadership success comes not just from being liked but from being respected and trusted—what can be termed as "liker-ship." Liker-ship is when a leader is well received and respected by their constituents. They are a new, bright star in the eyes of others, one who has also garnered the trust needed to move an organization forward. However, liker-ship can be temporary.

Transitioning into a leadership role, whether internally or externally, involves earning respect from your constituents. Respect isn't handed out freely; it's earned. While new leaders may find this challenging, even seasoned leaders grapple with maintaining respect. It's difficult, but it's necessary for leadership survival. Earning respect paves the way for trust, and trust fuels motivation. Leaders must prioritize gaining the trust of colleagues, employees, boards, and communities. Trust can be lost just as easily and quickly as it was obtained.

Leveraging respect and earning trust must start early and must be a continued focus. A proactive approach is crucial, laying the groundwork for successful leadership. True leadership goes beyond liker-ship; it involves not only being liked but also being trusted and respected. Leaders who command respect can effectively motivate and train their workforce, as we are more likely to be motivated and empowered by leaders we like.

Accomplishing respect and trust during your early leadership is vital to success. However, maintaining liker-ship is not an easy feat—it can be lost quickly if a leader is not careful, so it must start early and remain a priority.

Liker-ship has a wide-reaching impact on organizational success, and it will be at odds with leadership when unfavorable and difficult decisions are made. Sometimes, a leader will have to give priority to things other than being liked by others. Even though a decision may have been made in the best interest of the organization, it was not a fan favorite, and the lever of the likability scale decreases. There will inevitably be times when you will have to make an unpopular decision, but you can recover.

You can have liker-ship and leadership simultaneously, but liker-ship is not a prerequisite for leadership. It does, however, lay the foundation for leadership success. Transitioning liker-ship to leadership is an emergence. One must let go of past positions or roles in order to emerge. It takes coming out and letting go of that short season. It's like stepping into another realm of KNOWING.

With discernment and the right strategies, liker-ship can lead to productivity and longevity in leadership.

Principles of KNOWING

Many new and experienced leaders naively attempt to get around this period because they feel they already KNOW everything. During the honeymoon period, a leader must get to know themselves as a leader by determining their leadership style, but they must also examine their level of commitment. Are they in it for the short term or for the long haul?

True leaders understand that to ensure an organization's longevity and growth, they must lead from its very roots. A new or tenured leader must consistently examine and research every aspect of the organization. Knowing the history of the organization does not mean holding on to that history. Sometimes, holding on to history can impede your destiny. Know the history, but in order to move forward, focus on what is before you. Become fearless in the pursuit of honoring the past, but produce positive outcomes in the present.

Roots represent the foundation and anchor of any organization. Leaders who operate from this solid base provide stability and guidance as the organization transforms and evolves. Examine whether you want to lead from the top down or from the roots up.

In leadership, you must do more than *get* ready for an unknown journey; you must *stay* ready. Leadership is a journey that must begin with clearly defined stages filled with growth and learning. You must be ready to evolve. Each stage of the journey requires alertness and commitment. You must know what type of leadership journey you are navigating and how swiftly your journey can change. You must be aware of and ready for changes throughout the journey. Before instituting any change, a leader must have knowledge. They must be equipped with

- knowledge of self;
- knowledge of others;
- knowledge of their job;
- knowledge of the culture;
- knowledge of the organization's history;
- knowledge of the organization's structure.

Knowing will be one of the most powerful elements of leadership. It is the line drawn between success and failure. It is this element that allows a good leader to lay bricks in preparation for building a solid foundation.

KNOWLEDGE OF SELF

Effective leaders are distinguished by their acute self-awareness and recognition of their unique traits, styles, and nuances. This introspection is paramount in understanding and leading others competently. A leader's knowledge of their distinct leadership style is not just a reflection of self-awareness; it's a tool. It facilitates better collaboration, fosters improved relationships, and streamlines communication with others. By owning their leadership style, leaders can pinpoint their strengths and address their weaknesses with precision.

Before aspiring to guide others, leaders must first understand themselves. Several tools, like scales and tests, can help someone understand their own leadership style. These brief evaluations yield profound insights into a leader's emotions, values, personality, strengths, and weaknesses. Leveraging these results can assist leaders in identifying areas for improvement, enhancing communication skills, and fostering a deeper understanding of diverse perspectives.

Embarking on the leadership journey with a deep understanding of oneself sets a foundation for recognizing and valuing the diverse thoughts and actions of others. Such awareness not only catalyzes personal growth but also equips leaders to positively influence and shape the practices of their teams.

KNOWLEDGE OF OTHERS

Knowing and interacting with people at all levels is at the core of leadership. This can be really difficult if you do not know your key players. You have to learn others' personalities, and you have to motivate, train, build capacity in, and provide mentorship to them.

One of the most important aspects of leadership is knowing your team and partners. In order to be a leader, you need people to follow you. Knowing the different characteristics of your team members and partners will help build a sense of trust and respect within your organization. Knowing your constituents will allow you to carry out the organization's vision and mission.

Leaders should always get to know their staff members, boards, and community partners. When a leader is able to make connections with others, it leads to better performance by staff and stronger relationships with board members and community partners. A leader must open lines of communication to engage and interact with all constituents. Knowing your constituency will also help communication and listening skills improve. You'll be able to pick up on subtle cues and have a better understanding of your team.

Knowing helps build rapport, which leads to respect. In addition, it allows the leader to serve as a mentor and enhances the climate and culture. By knowing your constituents, you gain insight, which enables you to change behaviors and practices. The more you know and understand your team, the more they respect you and your direction for the organization. As such, performance and partnerships increase.

Many times, leaders fail because they begin by focusing on the outcome and not the process. Knowing others is a major component of the leadership process. You will never obtain the outcome without knowing those responsible for getting you there.

KNOWLEDGE OF THE JOB
Leadership undeniably stands as one of the most challenging roles anyone can undertake. Many leaders step into their positions without a comprehensive grasp of their job's intricacies and its alignment with the broader organizational vision.

However, with adequate preparation and understanding, a leader's journey can be both impactful and fulfilling. While every leader brings a unique blend of education, skills, and talents to the table, this knowledge base falls short without a thorough understanding of the specific leadership role they're assuming. It's imperative for leaders to have a deep knowledge of the organization they're serving. Before anyone takes on a leadership role, preliminary research on the company and its track record is beneficial. Yet, once in the position, leaders must delve deeper, understanding not just the role but also its significance within the organization's larger framework. This insight is crucial in making informed decisions and steering the organization with confidence.

A leader's understanding shouldn't stop at their own job; it's essential to grasp the roles of those around them. Official job descriptions, while useful, often only scratch the surface. Beneath them lie unwritten expectations and nuances critical to the job's execution. Leaders should exercise caution during their honeymoon phase. While differences from previous experiences or expectations might be evident, hasty changes can inadvertently disrupt the organization's culture and climate. Truly understanding a role goes beyond its formal description; it requires recognizing and adapting to the unspoken practices and behind-the-scenes functions that have proven successful.

KNOWLEDGE OF THE CULTURE

Leadership is not just about mastering the job but also about understanding the broader system and dynamics within which the job operates. Central to this is grasping the deep-rooted culture of an organization. Recognizing and influencing the cultural nuances is instrumental in driving the change needed for success. A robust organizational culture not only motivates but also enhances productivity.

A leader's approach and actions can significantly shape the organization's culture. Whether they succeed or falter, leaders continually mold the cultural fabric. It's crucial for leaders to consistently gauge the cultural pulse of their organization. They can do so in the following ways:

- Gather feedback from meetings – include a brief exit slip.
- Observe and gauge the feedback – take meeting notes.
- Walk and talk with stakeholders – provide consistent visibility and an open door policy.
- Be inclusive in decision-making – include stakeholders in strategic planning processes.
- Value employees – start an employee recognition program.
- Disseminate a brief climate survey – develop a survey instrument.

The early culture of an organization can break down for many reasons. A negative culture can impact a leader's ability to lead effectively, which can be detrimental to productivity and morale, ultimately resulting in high turnover. This type of culture can greatly harm the success of an organization. A negative culture can stem from many outlying factors, such as:

- misaligned values – a leader must align their values with the workforce's beliefs;
- lack of communication – communication must be clear, concise, and implicit;
- inconsistent expectations – develop strong plans and clear directives;
- toxic environment – value and recognize employees and other stakeholders;
- lack of ownership – embrace inclusion in all aspects of the organization.

Your leadership could be faced with critical disruptions that cause a complete reversal of your leadership course early on. This could totally shatter your leadership ability if you are not prepared to shift and rewind. One of the most important things a leader can do to lead effectively when a culture goes left is to be prepared to change their leadership course.

KNOWLEDGE OF THE ORGANIZATION'S HISTORY
As a leader, you must be prepared to change the course of history. The organization cannot grow if you hold on to history. In the 21st century, change is at the core of everything we do. Technology modernization requires adaptability. As a result, leaders must build a change management plan that is grounded in history.

Successful leadership hinges on adept navigation through the complex currents of organizational change. This isn't just about altering visions or objectives. It encompasses modifying the surrounding environmental factors to shift behaviors and reframe the cultural ethos. Before steering the ship of change, leaders need to observe, engage, and familiarize themselves with the organization's legacy.

One approach to adaptable leadership is to leave the past behind and focus on the future of the organization. Leading organizational change will come with its own set of new structures and systems. There will be many in the organization who will resist change, as those who have been in the organization for a length of time may see change as something negative. The age-old adage "That's how we've always done it" will inevitably emerge when new ideas are tabled. Sometimes, holding on to history can cost you your destiny.

KNOWLEDGE OF THE GOVERNING BOARD

Governing boards are needed to set policies and to ensure the organization is meeting its strategic goals. Beyond understanding the organization's internal dynamics, it's vital to recognize the influence of governing boards. These boards seek assurance in the leader's capability to steer effectively. While having comprehensive knowledge of the organization is beneficial, it's impractical to know every minute detail. However, a mutual understanding between leaders and their boards is crucial. Boards are pivotal for an organization's success, and building rapport with them is essential for harmonizing diverse viewpoints and agendas.

KNOWLEDGE OF THE ORGANIZATION'S STRUCTURE

Organizational structure refers to how the organization functions from day to day. It's more than an organizational chart listing departments and people. It encompasses exactly how those departments and people function and how they are aligned with the vision of the organization.

As you step into the shoes of leadership, you must embrace the organization's structures, including its processes and operations. Knowing the organizational structure is key to success. Leaders, especially if they are new, must embrace and internalize the structure and key workings of the organization.

In order for an organization to grow, it must evolve, and as an organization changes, so should its organizational structures. Therefore, an organizational structure is forever evolving. A leader must have in-depth knowledge of the workings of the organization—where the gaps exist, the work processes, the departments, staffing, etc.

For a new leader embarking on a job amidst new and ever-changing organizational structures, it is essential to understand the systems and processes required for the survival of the organization. Before a leader can depend totally upon others to support their leadership, they must be "in the know" regarding how systems operate. The leader must have well-thought-out plans to meet the needs of the future, and these plans must be based on understanding and improving upon the systems and processes of the organization. The leader will write and rewrite their plans as they adjust to their new environment.

Knowing their organizational structure will allow leaders to

- close existing gaps;
- reorganize with precision;
- build capacity and mentor effectively;
- change staff;
- increase engagement.

A leader must improve the organizational structure to support growth and development and drive success. Strategic changes can have a positive impact on your long-term goals.

KNOWLEDGE AND WISDOM
Even at the pinnacle of leadership, it's a misconception to think one must know everything. Leaders are not robots; they are humans, and the human mind can process and hold only a limited amount of information. When you are overseeing an organization with various departments, it's okay to hire highly qualified individuals and allow them to lead their respective areas. However, the leader must learn and know enough about all respective areas to be in the know and drive success.

"I got this!" "I don't need anybody!" "I'm good!" These are phrases leaders tell themselves before they fail. Leadership can sometimes be a lonely journey, but no one can be successful in isolation. Even after you have become a leader and made it to the top, you still need support and mentorship, whether you are an aspiring leader or have been one for 20 years. All good leaders have someone they can call upon at any time, such as a support group of colleagues in their circle that continues to uplift each other.

It's okay to be in the top seat and still have a lot to learn. Most leaders don't know everything but continue to learn each day. Accept what you don't know, but continue to grow. Do not measure your leadership by what someone else is doing.

Leaders at all levels need to be supported. In order to grow and mature, you cannot rely on self-sufficiency; instead, be prepared to accept the knowledge and wisdom of others in the field. You may have made it to the top without help, but can you sustain your position when storms arrive?

Don't show up for the wrong war or fight on the wrong battlefield. In leadership, the war's outcome is decided by the power of your mind. You will need many strategies to fight and win the war.

When a construction team begins to build a skyscraper, they do not start by building upward. In fact, they start by digging down and developing a solid foundation. If you don't dig down, you can never build up. To build an organization, a leader must dig down to those deep-rooted issues.

Take a look at your new reality. You can't grow if you're stuck in an old reality. A fish's growth is determined by the size of its environment: in a tank, it can only grow so big, but if you place the fish in the ocean, its growth is limitless.

The Journey

As I entered the top job, I began observing and conducting learning walks with key staff. I determined that I had just stepped onto a boat and everyone was rowing in different directions. There was not just one boat, but multiple boats going in different directions. Some boats even seemed to be rowing but were not moving at all. Some were just sitting idly.

I somehow had to get everyone rowing together in the same direction. This was not going to be easy. I knew I had to act swiftly or jump overboard quickly.

I was faced with getting a multifaceted organization on the same page. During my honeymoon period, I was working with the board that hired me, and they were supporting my new ideas and directions. With all of my previous leadership experience (even though I had never been a superintendent of schools), I thought I could do this alone. I had been successful in four leadership jobs that led me to the superintendency. My thoughts were that if I'd had success with those jobs, it was inevitable I would have success at the next level. I soon learned that while I had the knowledge needed to take it on, I lacked experience in the cultural and political aspects of this position.

Though I had been avoiding offers of mentorship and support from new colleagues and professional organizations, I really needed it. Initially, I thought my success in previous leadership experiences was enough—I just knew those experiences would guide and direct me through this leadership experience. I soon learned the hard way.

I learned quickly after being consumed by a culture I neither knew nor understood. I rapidly discovered that collective bargaining units vary significantly across different organizations. This realization hit home after a vote of no confidence by unions who resisted change, despite not personally knowing me. Additionally, I underestimated the depth and intricacy of the political landscape in the educational arena, especially at the top level.

I was in the honeymoon stage, and this time, at this level, it was different. It was a tumultuous time, but I was in it for the long haul.

Cruise Ship vs. Battleship

The honeymoon is akin to a journey on a cruise ship. This period allows you to craft your leadership reality. This can include amazing experiences with enduring and impactful memories. While the honeymoon phase, much like a cruise, signifies relaxation and leisure, it's not devoid of challenges. However, these challenges often present "positive" stressors. It's a critical phase for setting the agenda; leaders should steer their own agendas, tailoring them to the organizational objectives. When your early leadership is in cruise mode, this is the time to set those foundational goals and lay down your leadership roots before the storm arrives. A good leader knows that the question is not *if* a storm will come, but *when*!

You will learn early on that leadership isn't always as glamorous as it may seem from the outside. The landscape of leadership is forever changing, and the driving force behind a good leader is knowing how to shift when the field changes. The calm cruise can swiftly transition to the tumultuous conditions of a battlefield.

Battleships symbolize war, equipped and fortified for conflict. Wars, intricate by nature, mandate exceptional leadership. It's imperative to nurture and train your team during turbulent times, for it's these times that truly reveal the mettle of your team. Your leadership response during these challenging times often sets the tone for prolonged success.

During a battlefield leadership, gaps may exist in the following aspects of leadership:

- forging alignments across the organization
- driving a vision and mission
- setting clear directions
- influencing others
- building trust

Battleships bear the marks of many skirmishes. As a leader, you must learn from these battle scars—they narrate your leadership journey. These scars not only chronicle past battles but also serve as lessons for future confrontations. Wear them as badges of honor and growth. How you perceive and leverage these scars can significantly influence your leadership trajectory.

It is in the midst of the worst battles that you fully realize your sense of leadership. Sometimes you get to choose your battles, and sometimes your battles choose you. When you choose your battles, choose wisely. Do not die on a battlefield that was not worth dying on.

Battlefield leadership is held together by routines, discipline, and a great plan. A great plan allows leaders to be ready and armed for any wars. Some battles you must engage, but you must do so by being prepared and having a plan. A forward-thinking strategy not only aids in navigating or winning battles but also armors leaders against potential pitfalls early in their leadership voyage.

Sometimes, avoiding the battle can be the best strategy, but following the strategic plan is key to your evolution. The plan will help leaders keep the organization's best interests at the forefront.

The Journey

> When I was a new superintendent, it was like boarding a cruise ship. I was able to work with the board that hired me and believed I was the right person for the job. The job, like a cruise, was initially adventurous, friendly, fun, flexible, impactful, and relaxed, and I met many new people. Like those who take cruises for the love of the ocean and travel, a leader in the cruise ship phase must have a passion for the work they do.
>
> I myself had just such a passion, both for the work I had done in the past and for the work I was embarking upon in the field of education. At the onset of my top leadership role, it was all that I thought it would be. However, that was short-lived. My environment quickly transformed from a cruise ship to a battlefield.
>
> Wartime brings about many stressors and deep depression. Many leaders fear this period. However, it is during these times that a leader grows in experience and in accomplishments.

In the educational realm, school districts are governed by boards of education, three or four members of which are elected every two years. Following my one-year tenure, an official school board election was held. Many candidates at that time were running on a platform that would undo everything the previous board had implemented—including their selection of the top seat.

I acquired many battle scars throughout my leadership journey. Initially, I was embarrassed by my scars and very uncomfortable talking about them. I felt they were degrading and preferred to pretend they never happened. I suffered tremendously.

Battle scars can be directly related to experiencing PTSD, because many battles are traumatic. The PTSD will trigger memories we are trying to avoid. The best way to overcome the PTSD acquired on the battlefield is to embrace your battle scars. Following much emotional stress, I finally chose to share my scars, and when I did, it was invigorating. It gave me a sense of freedom.

My ability to endure, to cope, and to overcome the difficulty associated with the battle I experienced was key in my growth and development as a leader.

As you remain in the honeymoon phase of the cycle of leadership, you should keep away from those stressors and disconnect from battles. You must be flexible and grounded, and you should stay focused on goals that will drive your leadership into the next phase.

Every leadership journey begins with a next step.

CHAPTER 3

GAINING MOMENTUM: POWER

"Don't confuse momentum with leadership. Leadership generates forward motion in the absence of momentum." —Brian Logue

When leading large organizations, you take on the daily task of not just building momentum but sustaining it. Every decision will ultimately rest on your shoulders, even if it is handed down from an external source or from a board of directors. Many times, these directives are seen as the enemy.

It is important to first acknowledge that becoming an effective leader takes years of engaging and serving in the position. As in any job, you learn by doing. Effective leadership is a lengthy process because there are many skills the leader must learn and acquire. In addition to learning and acquiring skills, leaders must also stabilize the organization's foundation, build morale, build relationships, embrace the organizational structure, and make connections.

Starting Power

Leadership is different for everyone. Do not predetermine what your leadership will be, or you will go into the position with false hopes and aspirations.

A new leader will inevitably inherit problems left behind by their predecessors—making it to the leadership realm is not a panacea. You must have a passion not only for the work but for seeing the work through, which means you must have an "ARE YOU SURE?" attitude:

- Are you sure you are committed?
- Are you sure you are up for a fight?
- Are you sure you can weather any storm that forms?

As you develop as a leader, you will become more reliant on yourself and your initial perceptions. In our early journey of leadership, we can drift like an airborne seed, tossed around wherever the wind blows. The seed blows around but may eventually become planted.

Like the drifting seed, leadership can be very fragile. You may not be able to make sense of what is (or isn't) going on. You may feel you've done everything right. You feel from your preconceived notions that your leadership should be taking a different direction, but, unfortunately, it is drifting. Your thoughts about leadership are shattered, and anxiety, doubt, and bitterness begin to surface. If you are going to have leadership longevity, you must move from *bitter* to *better*.

To transition from starting power to staying power, you must become more reliant on yourself and the reality of leadership.

Staying Power

Staying power refers to your ability to remain relevant as a leader while weathering storms. To have staying power, leaders must commit to employing multiple leadership strategies, and they must also become relevant. Relevancy creates staying power, but it requires constant reassessment of who the leader is and what they know they can do. Leaders should keep "I AM" statements close and refer to them frequently. These simple statements are designed for leaders to read and refer to before, during, and following their leadership experiences. These statements help the leaders remain grounded with respect to their true abilities and worth as a leader.

"I AM" statements serve as guiding beacons for leaders, anchoring them to their vision for the organization and aligning them with its goals. These affirmations not only instill pride and define priorities but also elucidate the motivations behind a leader's aspirations and their commitment to leadership.

Embracing and understanding these statements is essential, especially when navigating the multifaceted journey of leadership. Leadership, while rewarding, can be demanding, and having these statements as your touchstones can provide clarity during challenging moments. They act as steadfast reminders, ensuring that a leader's practices remain consistent and true to their core beliefs.

"I AM" statements encapsulate the standards and ideals that leaders should aspire to. Consider the following leadership affirmations as catalysts to harness your potential and elevate your leadership trajectory.

When you begin in or continue in a leadership role, introduce yourself to each of these statements by unpacking them. Leadership can beat you down, but having these statements handy can help you navigate the challenges along the way. These statements are guides that can be used to help leaders ensure their leadership practices are not wavering.

"I AM" statements:

- I AM all I can be.
- I AM a leader of people.
- I AM a producer of results.
- I AM a source of information.
- I AM a relationship builder.
- I AM a community builder.
- I AM a communicator.
- I AM the face and voice of the organization.
- I AM a provider and protector of resources.
- I AM a motivator.
- I AM the gatekeeper.
- I AM a constant learner.

This list is not exhaustive; it is fluid and based on one leader's experiences. You may add to or take away from the list regularly. The interpretations of these statements can vary; their power lies in personalizing them and subsequently internalizing their meanings. Your ability to stay in the game of managing a workforce will be determined by your knowledge of who you are and what you are capable of doing.

When you take a top seat, you must have confidence in what you can do. You must acknowledge the power that lies within. Realizing your "I AM" statements can help you keep your footing and stay relevant. Leadership will beat you down, but keeping and repeating these statements will assist you in staying grounded. The leader with staying power will be ready for change and adversity.

The leader with staying power will constantly communicate each stakeholder group's evolving needs and expectations to the other groups so that everyone can see how their work intersects with the overarching strategy.

Wonder-Working Power

When working with boards that governed my employment and the decisions I made, I initially yielded to who I knew I was. I was faced with a board that devalued my humanity. They sent a strong message that I was not worth much. This initially broke me and my opinion of who I was. I doubted myself and my ability as a leader. But in the midst of this adversity, I recognized that surrender was not an option. I had to rise, not just against the external challenges but also against the internal tempests of self-doubt. Determined to reclaim my sense of self, I began crafting daily affirmations, penning them onto Post-it notes that adorned my office walls. These words became my armor, helping me reconstruct my identity in defiance of the narrative others tried to impose on me. I had to create my own humanity despite what others were attempting to achieve.

The "I AM" statements evolved into an integral aspect of my leadership psyche. They bolstered my confidence, reinforcing my belief in my work and my purpose. Over time, these affirmations transformed from "I AM" to "I CAN," symbolizing my resilience and capacity to rise above negativity. This transition marked a phase of empowerment and rejuvenation in my leadership journey.

After months of persistent self-affirmation and introspection, I arrived at a profound realization: I was a leader not just by position but by destiny. Reaching the pinnacle of my career wasn't mere coincidence; it was a testament to my worth, resilience, and the unique value I brought to the table.

MO Power

MO Power is momentum in leadership. It's about putting and keeping things in motion and pushing the organization forward. A leader must have the ability to build momentum in order to achieve goals. To build momentum a leader must:

- know their job and the job they are asking others to do – you want to garner trust from your workforce, and knowing what you need to know will assist in building trust;
- build upon their own confidence – the more confidence a leader has, the more their staff respects their decisions;
- take pride in all aspects of their work – taking pride will become the model for excellence;
- stay consistently motivated – if you lose momentum, so will your workforce;
- form positive habits – remove negativity from your thoughts and actions. even when distractions surface, make every attempt to find something positive within a negative situation.

12 STRATEGIES TO BUILD MOMENTUM
Oftentimes the many stresses of leadership cause regression in momentum. When this occurs, the following strategies are helpful to regain organizational movement:

- Communicate effectively – Be clear and concise with information and directives.
- Be fair and consistent – Have the same rules and standards for all.

- Ensure a 24-hour feedback response time – Even if you cannot answer the questions, have a system in place to address employee concerns.
- Listen, listen, listen to employees – Just paying attention to employees can go a long way.
- Lead by example – Set positive, motivational examples.
- Communicate regularly and effectively – Noncommunication can be a sign of disrespect. No one wants to be disrespected.
- Provide respect and rapport – Get to know the people in your workforce and what is important to them.
- Provide growth and development opportunities – Employees are driven by the notion of upward mobility through growth and development.
- Include employees in the decision-making – Having a voice is important to employees; allow them to use it. Involve employees on critical teams.
- Implement a recognition and incentive process – Recognizing your workforce is a sign of respecting what they do and affirming that their accomplishments are important to you and to the organization.
- Take a walk in their shoes – Frequently visit their work areas.

THE MO EXPERIENCE

Leaders are essential to the culture and climate of an organization. They must create an environment that stimulates motivation. After momentum is established, a foundation is set for leaders to further motivate their teams in order to guide them to success.

The power of a highly motivated workforce cannot be overstated. Such a workforce consistently delivers top-tier performances. Furthermore, when motivation thrives, happiness usually follows suit. A contented workforce not only is dedicated but also takes immense pride in its achievements.

At this juncture of motivation, leaders can afford to take a step back. The need to micromanage dwindles, second-guessing becomes rare, and there's less of a requirement to revamp underperforming staff. A motivated workforce grants leaders the privilege to cede control, offering staff greater freedom and autonomy, and thus increases morale.

Morale can have a tremendous impact on motivation. It signifies staff satisfaction, trust, and engagement. When it increases, so do attitudes and productivity. It allows for staff to feel valued and ultimately improves workplace experiences.

The trifecta of momentum, morale, and motivation serves as a pathway to transformational change—the kind of change that promises sustained success. However, such profound change only materializes when leaders demonstrate purpose in their actions. They must be resolute in reshaping the organizational culture and in motivating employees toward the shared goal of propelling the organization forward. True leaders catalyze transformational change, ushering in a new era of momentum, morale, and motivation that will lead to organizational mobility. The following is a model for building sustainable growth through organizational mobility:

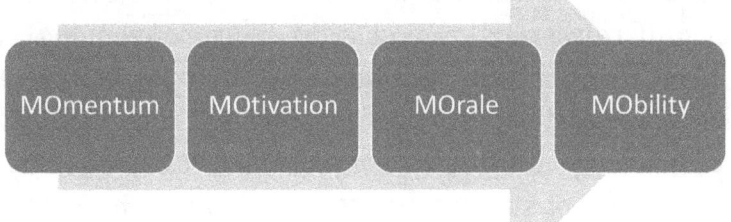

When a leader knows how to reach their full potential and how to get their team to do the same, they create a "MO" experience.

MO Better Blues – Finding the Pulse

Throughout my leadership journey, the state of employee morale consistently emerged as a pivotal indicator of our collective progress. In my inaugural leadership role, I grasped a foundational truth: motivation was a two-pronged challenge. While kindling my personal motivation was essential, sparking that same drive in others was equally paramount. I realized that maintaining my spirits was a prerequisite for inspiring and elevating those around me.

My early insight into building morale came from creating a positive climate and culture. This entailed taking the pulse of the organization's feelings and actions. A great leader never takes their fingers off the pulse of the organization. Numerous factors can potentially undermine morale, including internal distractions, gaps in communication, opaque policies, and feelings of alienation.

As the newly hired superintendent of a well-established, medium-sized school district, I walked into the midst of nearly 350 employees who had lost their momentum. The once high-performing district lost its momentum due to high turnovers among board members, senior-level positions, and other staff. I discerned a palpable disengagement among board members, mirrored by plummeting employee morale. Key stakeholders and partners were increasingly disillusioned by the district's declining performance metrics. It was evident that the taste of success had eluded them for an extended period of time.

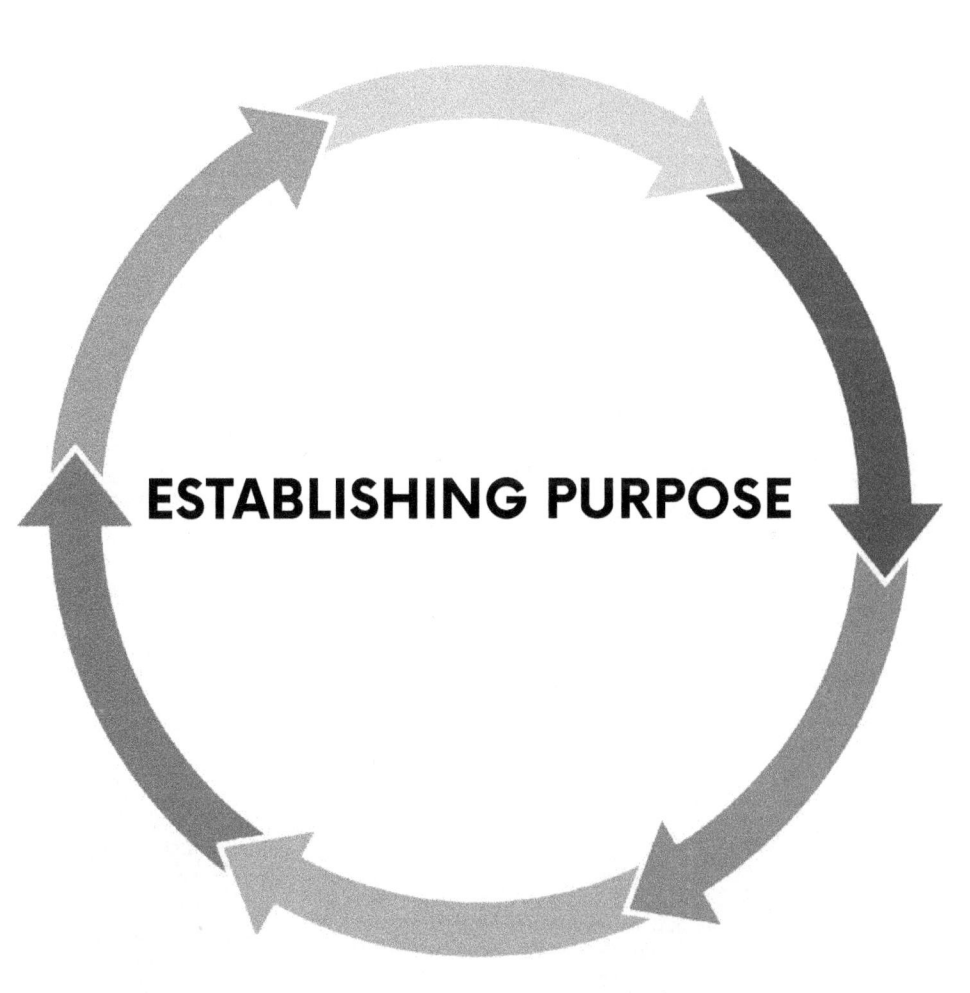

CHAPTER 4

LEAD OUT LOUD – LIVING YOUR PURPOSE

"If you can't figure out your purpose, figure out your passion. For your passion will lead you right into your purpose." —Bishop T. D. Jakes

A leader should possess an unwavering passion for their work, surpassing that of anyone else within the organization. This passion ignites a purpose, guiding the leader to concentrate on their goals and inspiring others to achieve them. The essence of leadership lies in the discovery and pursuit of this purpose. While there are endless avenues for leaders to manifest their purpose, identifying it remains paramount.

Finding and Sustaining Your Purpose

Discover, develop, and share your purpose. Your purpose is not just to make yourself happy but also to cement your relevance in leadership roles and in life itself. If you feel as though something's missing in your journey, it might be the absence of a driving purpose behind your passion. Passion, a deeply valued trait, can resonate and inspire others when it's rooted in purpose.

Every leader must be guided by purpose, and that purpose must resonate through your actions. Finding your purpose in life is a never-ending cycle.

It's common for leaders not to know what they are passionate about. Many leaders enter professions unrelated to their passion. They also enter professions for the wrong reasons—money or prestige, for example.

Timing is also critical in determining whether you will be successful as a leader. Many leaders fail because it is simply the wrong time and their passion is just not there. Executing at the wrong time will cost them passion and purpose. Often, leaders create their purpose based on what others want from them, which can be detrimental.

A lack of passion or a misaligned purpose can lead to feelings of dissatisfaction and unproductiveness. Leaders should be vigilant about not being confined by someone else's vision of purpose, as each individual is uniquely designed for their distinct purpose.

Instead of actively seeking out your purpose, allow it to reveal itself to you. When it does, embrace it, irrespective of its popularity or current trends. The right leadership journey emphasizes and prioritizes this purpose.

The essence of leadership is purpose. It shapes the organization's mission, vision, values, and goals and should resonate with stakeholders. This purpose sets the direction for leadership endeavors and should be embodied in every facet of the organization.

Leadership purpose is about the leader and what will drive their leadership daily. Your leadership purpose can be summed up in brief statements about what is important to you, which will drive how you lead the organization. These statements are forever evolving and go through the following cycle of effectiveness:

Leadership Purpose Cycle of Effectiveness

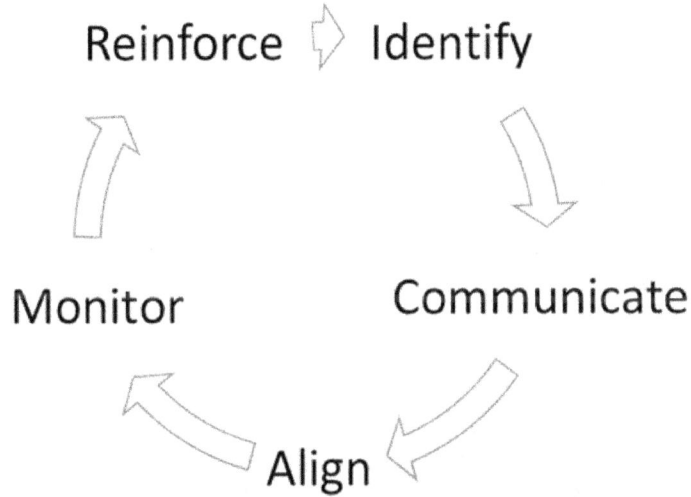

IDENTIFY

Every great leader must have an identified purpose to define them as a leader. Identifying your purpose will take much thought and will need to take the organizational priorities into consideration. The first step is to determine your WHY. Why will you do what you do each and every day? This will become your reason for leading and the core of your leadership.

COMMUNICATE

A great leader will inform others of the purpose through various forms of communication. The leader should create a communication agenda to ensure all information being shared about the purpose is accurate and consistent. By effectively articulating their leadership vision, a leader gains buy-in and support for carrying out the purpose. Communicating the leadership purpose provides consistent information about the purpose from the leader down through the organizational structure.

It will help the leader get the facts out, bring organizational consistency, and put the workforce on the same page.

ALIGN

Alignment is one of the most important aspects of the leadership purpose wheel. Deliberate alignment of leadership purpose across all organizational facets is essential for realizing goals and objectives. Such focused alignment not only streamlines systems and processes but also motivates and energizes the workforce to fulfill the overarching leadership vision.

MONITOR

Regularly monitoring your leadership purpose allows you to gauge whether it remains a paramount focus within the organization. Such vigilance aids leaders in discerning if the purpose is being upheld and aligned, or if your efforts are coming up short and you will need to make revisions or updates to your purpose. This will provide for organized, regular, consistent, and planned checks on purpose effectiveness.

Monitoring your purpose will create opportunities to reflect on it, receive feedback, and clarify it. This proactive approach empowers you to make well-informed decisions and ascertain the achievement of your intended outcomes.

REINFORCE

The purpose you set as a leader is instrumental to the organization's success. Hence, periodic reinforcement of your leadership purpose becomes essential. Reinforcement allows you to revisit, rethink, and revise your leadership purpose. It's important to recognize when your purpose needs reinforcement:

- There is a misalignment between your purpose and the organization's mission and vision.

- You have a sense that the purpose isn't setting the stage for success.
- The organizational outcomes are falling short of your goals.
- The purpose no longer supports the development of the organization.
- Your WHY has changed due to organizational shifts.

If the purpose of the organization is not held as sacred, the organization will be disjointed.

Drafting My Own Narratives

> A leader must draft their own story and become the author of their own fate. A well-developed story can be the impetus for garnering respect as a leader. Leaders who tell their own story are valued.
>
> Before I could draft my own narrative, I had to determine what great leadership looked like. I found myself leading people who were going in different directions, with different agendas, in many different locations, and who lacked information and development.
>
> Not fully understanding my purpose allowed others to tell my story. The stories told about me and my leadership were negative in nature, circulated by those who did not appreciate my leadership decisions or who had a bad experience at one of the school sites I led. The extent to which people could distort reality and spread malicious tales was a revelation to me.

When leaders don't actively share the achievements within their organizations, they leave room for outsiders to craft the narrative. One particular board member was relentless in spreading misleading stories about both my leadership and the district's success. She resisted change, wanting everything to remain static. Her false narratives were being released because my new leadership style was not in line with past practices or personal agendas. Soon, she influenced others into adopting and echoing her false narrative.

My reputation was being tarnished both in formal publications and on social media platforms. Recognizing this, I realized the importance of controlling my narrative to ensure it was conveyed clearly, consistently, and accurately.

In response, I transformed an existing role into a communications-focused position, tasking the individual with the responsibility to consistently "Tell Our Story." We proactively disseminated our narrative through various media channels, from creating regular newsletters for the community to attending local meetings. Embracing the power of social media, we showcased the exemplary work of our schools. Additionally, we fostered constructive relationships with local newspapers and broadcasters to ensure our accomplishments were highlighted.

By implementing these measures, I managed to get the right information to the right people at the right time. This allowed me to center my energies on advancing the organization. While the unfavorable narratives didn't disappear entirely, their prominence was significantly diminished.

Leadership Pledges

A leadership pledge is a promise that leaders make to themselves and their team. It serves to illuminate the leader's core values and priorities, thus guiding the organization toward its desired objective.

Leaders must motivate their staff to buy into their vision. A pledge is a commitment and a call to action—action that will change our thoughts, behaviors, and practices. A pledge without action is just a quote without meaning.

A leader can use pledges in the workplace to drive their purpose. Some pledges incorporate motivational cues that translate into decisive action. This can bolster productivity and align individuals more closely with the organization's overarching goals.

Pledges can make your purpose a priority. These commitments should be deliberate, always pointing toward the organization's vision. When upheld consistently, pledges can have a long-term impact on a person's performance and enable them to unleash their passion while staying focused on the purpose.

LEADERSHIP PLEDGES

- **Move away from first base**; you can't win the game otherwise.
- **Stay visible** to be accessible and have the ability to see all practices.
- **Keep the main thing, the main thing** until it is no longer the priority.
- **Ignite your passion** daily and allow others to see your light shine.

- **Set high expectations** for yourself and never lower them for anyone.
- **Challenge the status quo**, but be prepared when it challenges you back.
- **Share your thoughts, actions, and deeds**; they are no good when you keep them to yourself.
- **Don't walk alone**; we can go further and faster together.
- **Commit to your vision**; that commitment will see you through success.
- **Commit to transformational action** to protect and grow your brand.
- **Take bold steps** until you reach the finish line.
- **Make intentional choices** that will benefit the organizational goals.
- **Never hesitate** to do what is just and what is right.
- **Have the courage to lead** with resiliency and empowerment no matter what may come your way.
- **Be steadfast and unmovable** when it comes to carrying out the ideas and goals of the organization.

From Pledge to Progress

The pledges became my badge of honor. I repeated certain pledges daily, internalizing them and making them a part of my daily practices. These were like affirmations. They changed my mindset and behavior, allowing me to stay focused and prioritized in thought and action.

In over 30 years of leadership experience, these pledges have been invaluable. They have not only informed my decisions but also bolstered my confidence to take risks, knowing that I was doing the right thing.

The higher you climb up the organizational ladder, the more your leadership will be challenged. In leadership, you are responsible for a multitude of resources, including financial ones. During my tenure, there were times when I was asked to engage in illegal practices. But with my pledges as my compass, I remained unwavering in my commitment to the vision and mission I had for the institutions under my care, always choosing the path of integrity.

Crafting these leadership pledges wasn't just an exercise in self-assurance; it was a testament to my unwavering dedication to the schools I was entrusted with. Embracing them as affirmations reinforced my beliefs and ensured that I stayed true to my ambitions and objectives.

Becoming an A-Lister

Leaders are a dime a dozen, but those who truly shine focus unwaveringly on the WHY of their leadership. Understanding your purpose hinges on recognizing and embracing who you are as a leader.

The subtle actions of a leader can speak volumes about their purpose. You must aspire to be an A-list leader by coordinating your actions accordingly. An A-lister is ambitious, encouraging, supportive, inspirational, and appreciative.

What sets an A-list leader apart? They exhibit an unmatched dedication to their role and organization. To either attain or sustain this revered status, there are distinct attributes a leader must encapsulate. Here are some defining characteristics that every remarkable leader embodies to fuel their purpose:

- Ambitious – A great leader must possess alpha personality traits. Characteristics such as determination and ambition are key.
- Attaining – Leaders are never done learning and always seek to improve themselves.
- Approachable – Leaders must possess a certain self-confidence that allows them to listen to and value the opinions of others.
- Aware – You must know what you know. Knowing what is going on around you is foundational. Without knowledge, your leadership is dead. You will reap many benefits and rewards from being absolute in what you know.
- Adventurous – Step out and take some risks. Even good things can be risky. Risk-taking can elevate your leadership.
- Active – Actively engage in communicating and listening. Communicating is a two-way street. Be willing to look, listen, and learn.
- Accountable – Accountability begins with you. Own it! Be up for the challenge and own it from start to finish.
- Authentic – A leader should have a servant's heart. Show your authentic self at all times, ensuring that people see you for who you truly are.
- Absolute – Be deliberate and intentional in your actions and approaches. This requires planning. Actions driven by intentions will bring purpose and meaning to your leadership.

A-listers will consistently use the above list, which reveals some essential truths about leadership direction, to reflect on their WHY.

Your leadership WHY is about how you ensure your values are kept sacred. It defines what is paramount in your professional journey. It's also about your WHY statement—what motivates you, what matters to you, and what drives you to do this work.

Aligning your WHY with these A-list attributes not only defines you as an elite leader but also roots you in confidence and self-assuredness. A-list leaders exude self-confidence and appreciate the contributions of others.

The A-list is an automated, anywhere, and anytime collection of attributes possessed by good leaders. No single attribute is more important than the others. They are all essential to finding and being your true leader self. They hold the key to finding your purpose.

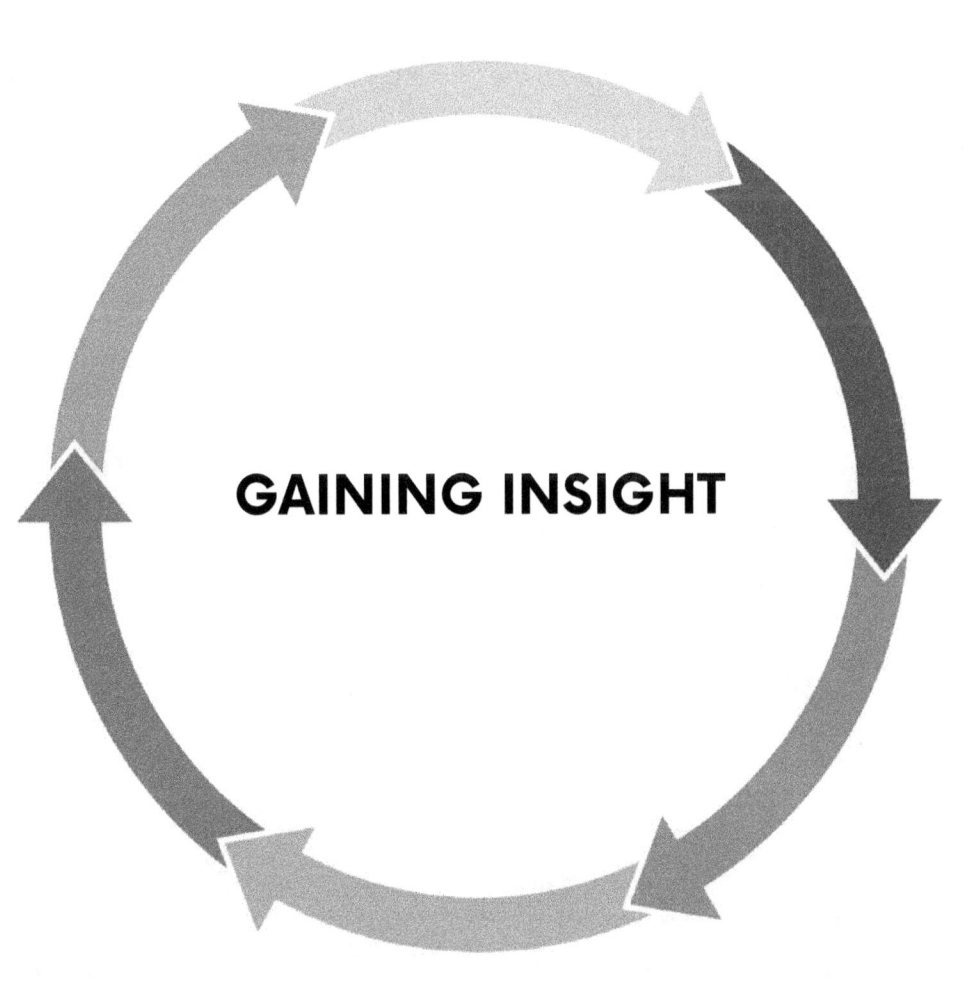

CHAPTER 5

INSIGHTFUL LEADERSHIP

"The best vision is insight." —Malcolm Forbes
*"Learn from yesterday, live for today and
hope for tomorrow."* —Albert Einstein

A leader must have a clear sight of their leadership at all times. This clarity is what empowers them to navigate their journey with confidence and purpose.

The hallmark of successful leaders lies in their ability to be profound thinkers and listeners. They rely not just on external insights but also on their internal compass to guide their actions and reactions. These inner deliberations become the backbone for pivotal conversations and decisions.

Leaders are faced with an array of challenges. Regardless of your level of experience or your field, it's this lucid vision—often referred to as instinct—that becomes a cornerstone of success. It's crucial to recognize these instincts and channel them into constructive dialogues, actionable suggestions, discerning decisions, and solid recommendations.

You know a good leadership instinct when it hits you. This leadership trait can make a real difference. A good instinct will grab your attention, enabling you to boldly think beyond the immediate issues, look at the big picture, make connections, move forward on new ideas, and consider alternative solutions.

Gaining Insight

Insight is a profound understanding that transcends surface-level knowledge. It offers individuals a deep grasp of themselves, others, and situations, and it can imbue leadership with purpose and depth.

To make solid decisions, it's essential to harness one's insight. This profound understanding aids in navigating intricate issues and unlocking the constraints of leadership. Insightful leaders are perpetually generating fresh ideas and perspectives, which can emerge spontaneously or be the result of deliberate contemplation.

Insight can be a flash of revelation—an unmistakable "Aha!" moment. It shares a kinship with instinct, stemming from an inner reservoir of understanding. Both are unyielding forces that shape our thoughts and decisions. Recognizing and trusting these internal guides is pivotal for a leader, and adapting to their spontaneity is part of the leadership journey.

The path to exemplary leadership isn't instantaneous; it's an evolution. Insight serves as a linchpin in this developmental process, propelling leaders toward heightened understanding and effectiveness.

Insight and knowledge are intrinsically linked. You cannot truly possess one without the other. Insight encompasses a profound understanding of one's role and the ability to disseminate this comprehension to others. It's the foundation upon which informed decisions are built. While young leaders might initially grapple with limited insight due to unfamiliarity with their team, organization, or protocols, their depth of insight will be augmented as they mature in their roles.

Leaders with a keen sense of insight combine their instincts and empirical evidence to celebrate successes and address missteps. For transformative change, decisions should be rooted in both insight and concrete facts.

Your destiny depends on your sight as a leader. A person who lacks insight is closed-minded and lacks vision and direction. A leader must know the power of their sight in order to grow.

A leader's sight furnishes them with knowledge and understanding about people, places, and things. Embracing insight invites innovative ideas and facilitates problem-solving.

Every leader, no matter their respective business, must be results driven. Without results, a leader can't measure their worth or success. Being a leader means navigating your organization toward its goals without losing touch with your identity and purpose. This entails not losing sight of who you are and why you are leading the organization.

In order to keep the WHY in your line of sight, you must use foresight, insight, and hindsight consistently throughout the leadership journey. Wise leaders use these three abilities all the time. Employing foresight, insight, and hindsight means being aware of your WHY at all times. Wise leaders use these concepts intuitively before, during, and after "an experience." Having great foresight, insight, and hindsight allows leaders to take control of their leadership.

To transform any organization, a leader must have sight of what is going on and be able to determine ways to make it better. Having this sight will allow them to leverage their ability to lead in the best and worst of times.

Insight can make those "Aha!" moments possible and transform doubt into clarity. Insightful leaders are influential and trusting. Being open-minded facilitates insight, although it is often achieved through lived experiences, study, and research. The more you know, the more insightful you tend to be. Insightful leaders are able to see beyond the rose-colored glasses because they are operating on knowledge and facts. They are able to break glass ceilings and remove barriers that are keeping them from moving forward.

Insight is a very powerful tool in the hands of leaders. Insightful leaders immerse themselves in organizational intricacies, drawing wisdom not just from formal education but also from interpersonal interactions. Their keen observations pave the way for a balanced approach, integrating foresight and hindsight into their leadership style.

Poor insight leads to poor leadership performance, especially in crises. Insight, coupled with knowledge, sharpens a leader's crisis management skills, sometimes becoming the very hallmark of their leadership style. A deficit in insight, often stemming from doubt or inadequate knowledge, can stunt a leader's growth. Poor or nonexistent insight is caused by doubt and lack of knowledge, and it will prevent you from growing or even surviving as a leader.

To acquire insight, one must seek knowledge and understanding. While the absence of insight can impede a leader's progress, there's always an avenue for rejuvenation. Through accumulated experiences and continuous learning, leaders can evolve. This evolution requires four actions:

- **Understand** – Navigate leadership with insight as the compass.

- **Know** – Have the pivotal self-awareness that allows one to comprehend one's traits, emotions, and thoughts.
- **Connect** – Channel inner reflections into actionable insights.
- **Trust** – Believe in oneself and one's instincts, accepting them as viable insights that inform leadership.

Epiphanies

Change requires leaders, whether new or tenured, to capitalize on their insight.

As change agents, leaders must use their intuition, instincts, and gut feelings to drive transformational change.

An epiphany is an abrupt or sudden awareness that a leader gains through an experience, which gifts that leader with new ideas, a needed change, a comprehension, or a lesson that will direct the leadership path.

Epiphanies arise amid everyday practices and bring about insight that can affect the way you lead. Embrace epiphanies and use them to guide and improve your practice. In my long leadership journey, I capitalized on those discoveries, revelations, and sudden thoughts and ideas. They became crucial to my survival and assisted me in evolving through the leadership journey.

Great leaders do not hold on to their epiphanies by keeping them to themselves; they share them and get others to buy into them, too. Epiphanies come from insightful leadership and evolve in the form of insight, foresight, and hindsight.

Foresight

As humans, we are creatures of the known. Tomorrow will have to come for us to think about it critically. Accordingly, great leaders spend more time thinking about past events than about current or future events—but it's important to think about these things, too. Leaders could not survive without planning or developing a vision for the organization.

Leaders must spend time exploring and concentrating on tomorrow, which sometimes takes a back seat to yesterday's and today's challenges. I see foresight as preparing for future challenges. It does not aim to predict the future but to predetermine directions for the future. Foresight helps leaders consider that what is yet to happen is just as critical as what has already happened. It requires us to lean into the unknown while learning from the known.

Whether you are a leader of today or tomorrow, no matter your field, adopting a foresight-oriented mindset is indispensable, as this will affect your choices, decisions, and performance.

Hindsight

Hindsight is invaluable in the leadership process. It entails looking back and reflecting upon your words, actions, and decisions. By revisiting our experiences, we can learn from our mistakes and successes and use that knowledge to help us correct behaviors in the future.

At its core, hindsight encourages a leader to continually assess the significance of past events. It nurtures the habit of questioning oneself, fostering a commitment to perpetual improvement. While predicting the future might be a challenge, understanding the past is often more straightforward, thanks to hindsight.

In leadership, cultivating the skill of hindsight is akin to honing one's reflective abilities. Effective leaders possess the capacity to review situations retrospectively, delving deep into past choices and seeking pathways for better outcomes. Just as insight illuminates the present, hindsight should be a daily practice, shedding light on the lessons from yesterday.

Leadership hindsight enables you to lead with the conviction of understanding the examples of the past, which allows you to demonstrate what you can do to improve outcomes and to grow from the experiences.

Sight Unseen

In my leadership journey, I've always been a forward thinker, which ensures that I'm equipped to handle both the challenges and the opportunities that come my way. This proactive approach has often opened doors to unique and innovative possibilities.

A significant part of my leadership strategy revolves around my epiphanies—those flashes of insight and intuition that seem to strike out of the blue. I've never shied away from sharing these moments with others, for they have been instrumental in navigating my path to success. To me, these epiphanies feel like divine interventions—unexpected yet profound moments that have steered my decisions and shaped my leadership.

Reflecting on these insights, I realize the depth of understanding they've imparted and the growth they've fostered in my leadership journey. Time and again, they have provided lessons that resonate deeply, molding me into a more focused and effective leader. These intuitive moments not only have enlightened me about the intricacies of organizations but have also been catalysts for change and transformation, influencing both my professional and personal lives.

The unpredictable nature of these epiphanies is what makes them so special. They don't operate on a schedule. Often, they've graced me during the most ordinary moments—perhaps when I'm immersed in thought or merely humming a tune while driving. Yet each revelation has left a significant mark, propelling me further on my leadership path and often sparking a cascade of related thoughts and actions.

What truly magnifies the impact of these moments is sharing them. Discussing these flashes of insight with others often brings new dimensions of understanding. Converting these intuitive moments into actionable steps has allowed me to ideate, perceive situations anew, address concerns, and resolve challenges consistently.

So I urge you to cherish and embrace your "Aha!" moments. They're not just fleeting thoughts but potential game-changers. If harnessed, they can pave the way for transformational experiences.

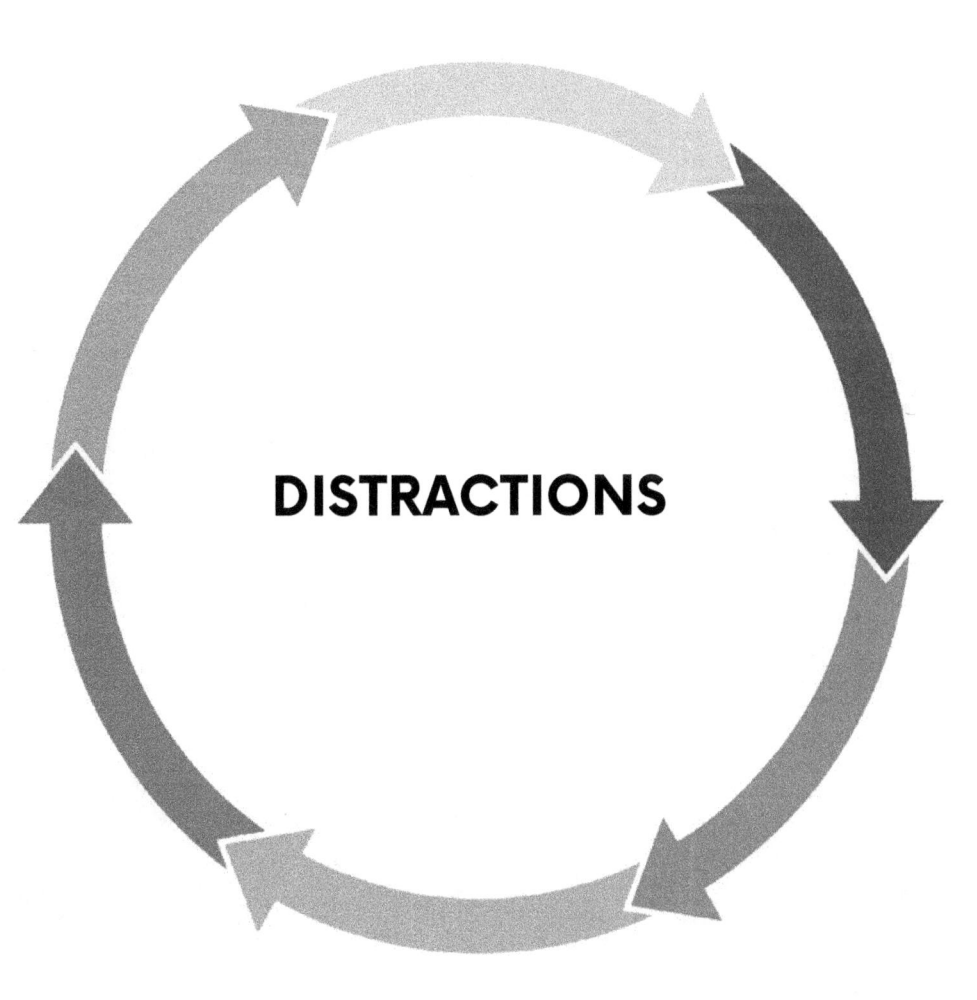

CHAPTER 6

THE MANY SHADES OF DARKNESS

"When you're going through hell, keep going." —Winston Churchill
"Only in darkness can you see light." —Jocko Willink

Darkness comes in many shades, and leadership will not always be bathed in bright light. As a matter of fact, darkness is inevitable, though often unexpected. A leader must be willing to lead and thrive through the good days and the dark days alike.

One of the most challenging aspects of such dark periods is the emergence of distractions. An effective leader's strength lies in their ability to concentrate their resources—be it influence, intellect, or inspiration—toward a singular, overarching purpose. However, when a leader is plagued by distractions, this potency can be critically diminished.

Distracted leadership results in a scattering of attention, with efforts dispersed thinly across a myriad of pursuits. This lack of focus can cause leaders to veer away from their main objectives and become entrapped in inconsequential endeavors. Whether these distractions are overt or subtle, their impact is consistently detrimental. They serve as barriers, deterring leaders from the trajectory of success.

Thus, recognizing and addressing these diversions becomes paramount. By doing so, leaders can continue to move forward, even when the path is shrouded in darkness.

Leadership in Despair

The journey of leadership isn't immune to moments of desolation. This state of despair can be a daunting vortex, plunging leaders into feelings of fear, melancholy, rejection, or even depression. Such phases, though unwelcome, are occasionally unavoidable.

Desolation doesn't discriminate between turbulent times and serene ones; it can emerge amid both tempests and rainbows. The triggers can be manifold, stemming from both internal struggles and external pressures. However, irrespective of its origin, it's crucial for leaders to possess the resilience and skills to confront this despair directly—and then bounce back. You can fall deeper into despair if it is not addressed.

The ramifications of a leader's desolation extend beyond personal torment. It can reverberate throughout an organization, influencing the morale and productivity of the workforce. Hence, it becomes imperative for leaders to swiftly harness their inner fortitude to confront, alleviate, and transcend such phases of desolation. My personal trysts with despair came from a combination of my own poor decisions and those made by the governing body overseeing my role. Despair came from trying to please too many entities and not staying focused on the purpose. At other times, it came from the stressors and frustrations that come along with a high-profile leadership position.

Regrouping, Rearranging, and Reflecting Through Darkness

There is no such thing as a leadership without storms. Dark epochs in leadership can be labyrinthine, yet they often present the most profound lessons and pivotal growth opportunities. Paradoxically, these trying times might offer insights richer than the most esteemed leadership courses at a university.

Leaders must enter their respective jobs knowing and understanding that storms may come and thinking about how they should react when they do. Equipping oneself with robust strategies is essential for such eventualities.

As leaders, we must be alert for impending storms. When you see the horizon darkening, you should hope for the best but be prepared for the worst. Like a seasoned meteorologist, you must know the signs. Recognizing a brewing crisis and orchestrating preemptive measures can often mitigate its impact.

The setbacks inherent to these storms can also be reframed as platforms for remarkable comebacks. It is the leader's responsibility to guide the way through the storm and to emerge stronger after it has passed, ready to thrive in the aftermath.

Although the word "storm" has a negative connotation, a storm can be a positive situation. While some storms (like hurricanes, tornados, typhoons, etc.) will kill and destroy, other, smaller storms can help the environment. In the same way, small challenges can benefit the culture of an organization.

No matter how disgusted or dismayed you may be, don't wave the white flag. Do not run out and leave great talent on the table because of a difficult journey. There is always a rainbow following a storm.

Resilient leaders stand their ground even in the fiercest tempests. They bear the weight of responsibility, internalizing their role as problem solvers. When crises emerge—be they financial, cultural, environmental, or academic—it's imperative to respond swiftly and effectively.

To manage these crises, leaders must adopt the "RE Play Strategies," which serve as a compass during turbulent times. These strategies, pivotal to a leader's arsenal, will be indispensable during unforeseen challenges. As storms are cyclical in nature, having these strategies at one's disposal ensures clarity and resilience through each tempest.

RE PLAY STRATEGIES:

RECHARGE – REFLECT TO GROW
You must regain energy to face challenges. This may involve taking a step back to refocus your lens so that you can see a bigger, clearer picture of your organization. Recharging could involve many **re**dos, such as **re**thinking, **re**building, **re**imagining, **re**vising, **re**creating, and **re**launching.

When the vitality of your passion is gone, you must recharge. If your vulnerability has a greater presence in your work, you must recharge.

RETHINK – INCREASE YOUR KNOWLEDGE
During storms, that which is normal becomes abnormal, and one must increase one's thinking. This is a time to use forward

thinking to rework operations. Rethinking is not recreating the wheel but embracing uncomfortable truths.

To rethink is to increase your knowledge by thinking outside the box and modifying or enhancing existing practices. Allow your creativity and innovativeness to drive true change and effectiveness following challenging times. Be prepared to revive existing operations, your culture, and your staff with forward-thinking strategies that align with your current goals, policies, and procedures.

REBUILD – BUILD RELATIONSHIPS AND TRUST

The first step in getting to know your stakeholders is to build sound relationships. Sound relationships are the foundation on which great leaders stand. Leaders must begin to develop respect for and rapport with all stakeholders.

Relationship building involves trust. Trust is a byproduct of these robust relationships, adding depth to your work and fostering productivity. Trust lends itself to communication, and communication to productivity.

RETOOL – REVISE THE SYSTEMS AND PROCEDURES GUIDING THE ORGANIZATION

Retooling involves revising the systems and procedures that guide the organization. Policies and procedures are the roadmap for organizational effectiveness. When the systems for policies and procedures are strong, it provides protection for all stakeholders and establishes a framework for success.

You may want to revisit organizational policies and procedures or revise the organization's strategic plan. When you do so, remember your deliberate purpose. Sometimes, it takes heat and pressure to grow your leadership. Going through difficult times can propel you toward your purpose. It may take a little heat to pressure you to do better.

REIMAGINE – UNLOCK ORGANIZATIONAL POTENTIAL

What was once comfortable and secure can become a cycle of turmoil. Reimagining takes moving away from your comfort zone to engage new and innovative thoughts, ideas, and processes.

In the face of storms, you must reimagine your goals in order to achieve organizational success. This may entail taking a step backward and reflecting on what is working and not working. Take the time to delve deep into your short-term and long-term goals with the intention of reconceptualizing them to meet the needs of the organization.

RECREATE – ESTABLISH PURPOSEFUL LEADERSHIP FOR MEANINGFUL CHANGE

Don't stay on the boat too long. Know when to come out of it and find new land. Remember, the boat is your transportation to your destination. If you put too much faith in your leadership title and degrees, your boat will sink, and you may have to build a new one. The boat is the vehicle that helps us get to our destination. Do not take the journey for granted.

RELAUNCH – EMBRACE THE VOLUME OF CHANGE

Be prepared to change your structure and your mode of operation. Your structure is the transportation, not the destination.

Do not fear darkness. Just as literal darkness will surely come every 10 to 12 hours, figurative darkness will surely surface during your leadership. It is our natural inclination to fear darkness, but do not fear for too long. Don't give in to the dark days of leadership. Darkness can be overwhelming and will be exacerbated if you give in to it. Darkness has no power of its own.

Before the digital world exploded, cameras used film that had to be developed from a negative in the dark. When the film was completely developed, a clear, vibrant picture was produced.

The storm is either going to drive you or drown you. When the storms of leadership surface, a well-prepared leader will survive. People become comfortable with the existing structures, but just as a quarterback modifies plays at the line of scrimmage, leaders must be adaptable. The goals haven't changed; it's just that a new "RE" play has been added. If you are going to win the game, you must move the goal post.

What the Heavens – When the Agendas Don't Match

Dealing with governing stakeholders can be very difficult when agendas are different, resulting in problems in the organization. It will sometimes be hard to determine what is motivating their decisions, points of view, actions, or ideas.

Governing stakeholders will often choose their personal agendas over the progress of the organization. Many times, they will exploit their position for power and their personal agendas.

These individuals play pivotal roles, as they often hold the reins to policy, procedural, or financial approvals. Fostering deeper relationships with stakeholders and gaining a genuine understanding of their motivations and influences can equip you to steer them constructively. Trust, built over time, can modify their perceptions and actions to align with organizational goals.

Get to know your stakeholders and try to understand what is motivating them and their actions. Know their internal and external influences. Know which stakeholders support your ideas and agendas and which ones do not. Differentiate how you engage with stakeholders who have different ideas. Identify stakeholders who can influence your agendas and success.

- Stay focused – Do not lose sight of your goals. Stay confident and remain the ethical leader you know you are.
- Communicate consistently – Engaging key stakeholders can help to foster trust.
- Decide what you can accept – Work with your stakeholders and be objective in adapting to stakeholder ideas.
- Stay informed.
- Strategically manage the key stakeholders.
- Allow time for joint growth and development.
- Get ahead of potential conflicts.

In every leadership role, challenges are inevitable, but by employing effective strategies, you can transform these challenges into opportunities. Don't let these challenges overshadow your goals; instead, pivot and search for ways to turn them into pathways for growth and success.

Quiet to Chaos or Chaos to Quiet

When troubles arise, there is always a calm before the storm (though sometimes the storm comes before the calm). There are signs during the calm that can prepare us for an impending storm. The storm can also prepare you for the calm.

Some storms throughout your leadership are so violent that you can't handle them alone. It's crucial to lean on those who have weathered their fair share of storms and possess the experience to navigate through them. You cannot undertake this journey alone, and it's when you feel lost that you should seek guidance to avoid getting caught in the eye of the storm. The eye of a storm is the area of calm in the center of a tornado, hurricane, or cyclone. Only a few people have seen one and lived to tell about it.

Some storms can make you want to throw in the towel, but leadership storms can be teachable moments that help you stay on course in the future. If you keep driving through the storm, you will eventually pass through it. Know that storms are temporary, and remain steadfast in your leadership. This will help bring about the calm.

Just as meteorologists utilize advanced tools and techniques to predict and track weather patterns, leaders must be equally vigilant in spotting early signs of potential challenges within their organizations. The ability to recognize and address these minor issues can prevent them from escalating into major crises. Being proactive rather than reactive is paramount in leadership, ensuring that potential problems are nipped in the bud before they grow into formidable storms.

Shades of Darkness – Taking Steps of Faith through Darkness

In order to find light in the midst of darkness, you must first understand why the darkness has come about. Darkness is part of a leader's reality. It is not a question of *if* darkness will come; it's a question of *when* it will come. Leadership will have its dark periods that come in many shades. If not adeptly managed, these periods can have devastating effects on both the organization and its leader. Such challenging phases can manifest as:

- distractions
- failures
- attacks
- hurts
- harassment

Darkness has always had a negative connotation. However, it's crucial to understand that not all periods of darkness signify hopelessness. In fact, many of these phases can serve as catalysts for innovation and growth. Some of our most remarkable accomplishments can emerge from these challenging times. Instead of dreading these phases, embrace them, knowing that after every night, dawn awaits.

Shades of Darkness

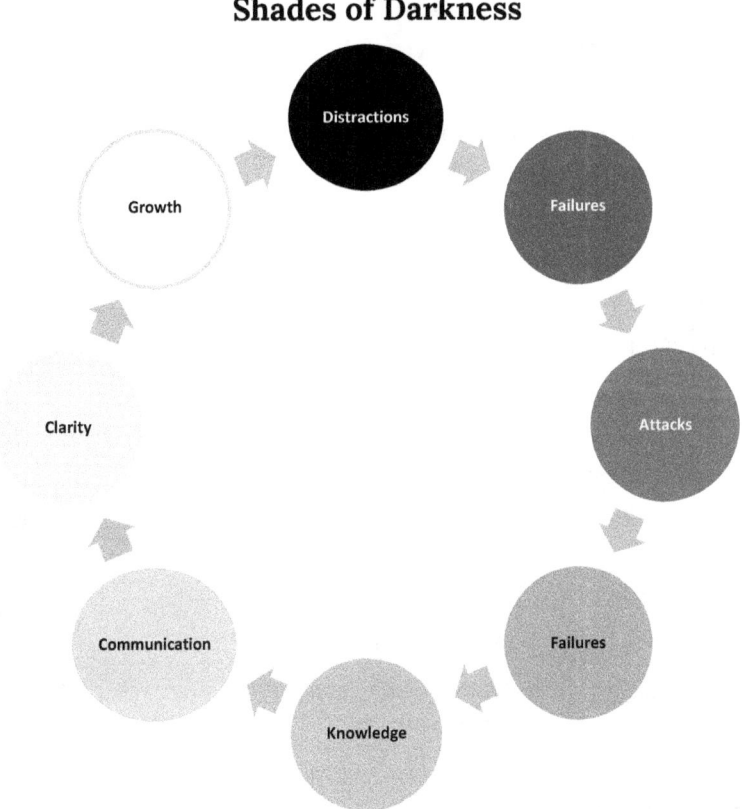

A dark period can provide access to many positives:

- knowledge
- newness
- clarity
- relationships
- a growth mindset
- communication

Without darkness, it is impossible to see the light.

If it were always light, we would never grow into the leaders we can be. Darkness allows us to focus on what is important.

There is no fixed time period or timeline for darkness; it will come and go throughout your leadership. Be prepared for those dark periods. Your responsibility as a leader is not to avoid these phases but to be prepared to navigate your way out of darkness back to light. There are many lessons to be learned from the darkness.

When Darkness Comes

I was able to recognize my despair early on. However, while acknowledging it is a crucial step, the real challenge is erecting defense mechanisms to combat those emotions.

A major storm gave me another chance. I learned through this tumultuous time that there can be great things on the other side of the storm: dry land, the sun, or a beautiful rainbow.

This storm came about as a result of a shift in the local political landscape. My honeymoon had ended, and the makeup of my governing board had shifted drastically. As a result of this change, most of the board was at odds with my viewpoint. They came with their own agendas.

The new governing stakeholders used their political power to attempt to discredit me and my leadership. This was devastating and plunged me into despair.

The despair during this storm affected not only me but also my leadership team. The people I relied on, with whom I'd shared the work of the organization, became so disenfranchised that they left to seek other jobs. I found myself doing the internal work alone.

My governing stakeholders and I came to a point where our agendas were just not compatible. This became an issue for me and my ability to lead and garner success. There was no way around having incompatible agendas or the negative consequences that resulted. However, while nothing could bridge the gap in our agendas, I was able to manage the stakeholders using some core strategies. These allowed me to move forward as I continued to oversee the organization.

In the midst of this storm—without a team—I leaned heavily on two colleagues and friends whom I admired greatly, both successful superintendents in their own right. One advised me that through the storm, I had to stay relevant. The other one urged me not to lose who I was. With their guidance, I learned to get ahead of such a storm. I also learned to be transparent about the crisis to maintain trust between myself and all the stakeholders.

After weathering a number of storms, I looked and listened, and learned a number of methods that enabled me to connect to this group.

In summary, the best way to manage stakeholders with different agendas is to

- communicate consistently;
- decide what you can accept;
- stay informed;
- manage the key stakeholders;
- prioritize joint growth and development; and
- address potential conflicts.

There were many dark days, but I had to carry on despite my circumstances. I had to own the dark days like I owned

> *all other days. I had an entire organization depending upon me as their leader. Even when the darkness was beyond my control, I stayed positive and motivated, and I remained engaged until I could see light again.*

Weathering the Storms – Learning to Dance in the Rain

Leadership isn't about having all the answers. The board or hiring officials do not hire you because you know everything. Many of them have very limited knowledge of the requirements of your position. They selected you based on your good communication skills, knowledge of the company, past experiences, and the dynamic presentation you gave. They were impressed by the plans you had for the organization.

Throughout any leadership role, there will always be some type of chaos. No matter what type of organization you lead, you can bet storms will form.

It's our job as leaders to identify potential problems early on. While some storms can be avoided, others are beyond our control. The key is to act swiftly, assess any damage, and implement repairs to prevent further issues.

There will be times when your leadership abilities are tested. It's crucial to have a lifeline, which can come in the form of a mentor or colleague—or else a book, an article, or even a workshop. These lifelines not only guide us but also mold us.

As we grow and benefit from these supports, we position ourselves to become invaluable lifelines for others in turn.

CHAPTER 7

BREAK EVERY CHAIN

"If you don't like something, change it. If you can't change it, change your attitude." —Maya Angelou
"Freedom is the power to choose your own chain." —Jean-Jacques Rousseau

Leadership comes with its share of distractions. These can impact the course of one's leadership and even become addictive. A leader's true strength lies in maintaining focus despite distractions. The essence of leadership is prioritizing the essential—keeping the main thing, the main thing. It's about keeping close those things you can change but letting go of the rest.

To stay on course, center your attention on what's within your control. There will always be things you can control and things you cannot. Don't try to manage what you can't manage. A leader will only make progress by keeping their leadership purpose true and at the forefront of all they do.

Leadership distractions, or chains, can come in the form of internal struggles such as anger, unforgiveness, lack of humility, or pride. These distractions will halt your leadership progress and stifle your capabilities as a leader.

Chains signify bondage of some sort. One can be bound by both visible and invisible means. Invisible chains can include guilt, shame, pride, greed, jealousy, hatred, negativity, hurt, or history, just to name a few.

Chains are barriers that prevent leaders from moving forward. Every leadership journey has invisible barriers. A leader struggles with these barriers because they are unseen, unheard, and intangible. These disrupting chains lead to skewed behaviors and decreased productivity.

Chains hold leaders back from reaching their full potential. Leadership is tough enough, but chains come to make us stronger.

Visible chains are easily recognizable chains that you can see:

- absent time management
- deficient self-management
- challenging employee relations
- difficult decisions
- perplexed board relations
- organization problems
- restrictive policies
- unclear procedures
- unrealistic timelines
- unclear communication/words
- personal agendas
- mixed messages
- unclear roles
- role complacency

Invisible chains are more detrimental than visible chains. These are stealthy chains that cannot be seen.

Great leaders will tackle the visible chains as well as the invisible ones. However, the invisible chains can be more difficult and problematic because they are unperceived. They are more subtle but can be even more restrictive. Leaders must have the strength and endurance to address these invisible chains throughout their leadership:

- fear
- doubt
- control
- power
- humility
- self-awareness
- pressure
- emotions
- judgments
- temperament

Chains will interfere with leadership, but they do not necessarily have to destroy it. Releasing or changing behaviors can positively impact your leadership.

Leaders often grapple with these unseen chains, as their stealthy nature makes them harder to confront. But acknowledging and addressing them is pivotal for growth, so great leaders must tackle and break ongoing chains.

Breaking chains can lead to freedom in leadership. Releasing or changing one's behaviors or practices can be a way of breaking chains. Some chains you will never break; you must learn to live with them and still be successful.

Breaking the visible and invisible chains will return power and direction to your leadership. A leader must be adamant and deliberate about breaking chains.

True freedom in leadership comes from breaking both visible and invisible chains. While some chains can be shattered, others must be managed or adapted to. Great leaders identify these barriers, confront them, and strategize to work around or overcome them. Through this ongoing process, they reclaim power and direction, guiding their leadership journey with renewed purpose.

Invisible Chains

After I had endured a challenging two-year leadership spell, a change in my board members marked a turning point. With a new board that shared my vision, I was presented with the opportunity to propel our organization forward without past constraints. However, the battle scars from my time with the former board remained, and I brought that trauma into my new leadership structure. I was continuing to agonize over what had happened to me to the extent that it was preventing me from building trust and partnerships in my new board of education. I had to gain the courage to let go of my herstory, which was becoming an invisible chain for me.

This past trauma had become an invisible chain, hampering my ability to trust and collaborate effectively with my new board of education. It was vital for me to muster the courage to release this weight, to not let my history dictate my present and future. These invisible chains included

- *resentment – I was unwilling to forgive the actions of others;*
- *pride – my pride was preventing me from accepting the things I could not change;*
- *offenses – I stayed on the offensive and challenged simple things;*
- *bitterness – I had lost my sense of humility and had become angry.*

This period was marked by invisible barriers that limited my leadership potential. These chains were not only pulling me away from my mission but also obfuscating my true destiny. Only by recognizing and actively addressing these chains could I realign with my purpose and lead with renewed vigor.

Breakthrough

To truly evolve as a leader, it's imperative to navigate through challenges, turning breaking points and breakdowns into transformative breakthroughs. This means proactively fostering change within your organization, adopting innovative ways of thinking, and ensuring lasting and sustainable progress.

Every leader will face changes and hurdles. The outcome can vary: either these events can culminate in frustration, causing detachment from the work, or they can catalyze breakthroughs, revolutionizing your perspective and propelling you toward success. However, achieving these breakthroughs isn't effortless; it demands a fresh approach, strategic decisions, and self-reflection.

A leadership breakthrough signifies attaining new heights in various facets—goals, challenges, or visions. To experience such advancements, leaders must broaden their horizons, equipping themselves for present and future challenges. Expanding leadership capabilities makes these breakthroughs attainable, ensuring you realize your utmost potential.

There are 10 identified strategies for unleashing the breakthroughs you are pursuing. These daily practices will evolve your leadership:

1. Communicate effectively – Ensure clarity and understanding in all interactions.
2. Expand knowledge – Dive deeper to amplify your impact.
3. Nurture relationships – Foster healthy dialogue and collaboration.
4. Champion teaming – Build professional, dedicated teams for optimal success.
5. Take a value-driven approach – Champion causes aligned with your core WHY.
6. Support the mission – Wholeheartedly endorse and advance the organizational mission.
7. Lead by example – Consistently embody the standards and values you advocate.
8. Set high standards – Aim for excellence in all organizational endeavors.
9. Practice self-reflection – Regularly introspect to gain insights and evolve.
10. Embrace authenticity – Align your leadership style with your intrinsic values and objectives.

Leadership Breakthrough

As the new leader, I started by leading from my heart. This approach allowed me to be myself because it aligned closely with my values. Heart leadership shows people that you care about the organization and about them.

Interestingly, it became clear early on in my career that this form of leadership was not working in the culture I had inherited. They feared change and felt I was coming to do what they were unwilling to do.

I knew I couldn't change who I was as a leader, but I had to employ another leadership style to accomplish my goals. Two things were happening simultaneously:

- My administrative team became more motivated and rendered better results.
- The majority of the employees had not embraced my style.

I found this to be very interesting. My leadership team accepted the approach, but the staff, for the most part, did not seem to embrace it. It was actually a tough path to navigate, and some critical decisions had to be made.

I realized that leading from the heart was not enough to produce the results that the district needed. I was too far removed from the masses, and my style was only reaching those I engaged most closely with. I realized that I simply had to share my knowledge and style with my administrative team so that the people they supervised and supported would benefit.

This leadership breakthrough came when I decided to stop doing what I had read in textbooks and to lead from my heart instead: making connections with people, getting close to them, really helping them to feel part of the leadership *process. I decided to show that I cared for them authentically, and that I would not compromise that.*

By following the above practices, I was able to break barriers and acquire breakthroughs that led my leadership and growth in a positive direction.

Such breakthroughs have been the catalyst that revived my journey and kept me going. Breakthroughs shaped and sustained my leadership over my long career.

I am sure that without breakthroughs, my leadership journey would not have stood the test of time.

Breakdowns

Breakdowns can be challenging and cause crucial hardship for one's leadership ability. Leaders must lead by example and have the ability to identify potential breakdowns. A team that lacks a strong leadership example will suffer greatly. A leader must be able to guide others based on their own actions and deeds. A leader must carry themselves in ways that demonstrate excellence. Excellence is not taught; it's modeled.

There are many warning signs leaders should be aware of in their search for success. A broken organization will have its fair share of difficulties and setbacks. Organizations strive to remain flexible and proactive, achieving long-term success through effective processes and systems.

For exceptional leadership, it's crucial for a leader to mitigate breakdowns in their administration. Ensuring that the organization's functions operate efficiently helps prevent potential disruptions.

COMMUNICATION BREAKDOWNS

Communication is a give-and-take situation. Effective listening is a crucial aspect of verbal communication within an organization. This two-way process requires the ability to hear the staff. They must understand the importance of their voice and its appreciation. Confusion is no friend of communication. Leaders must have messages that are clear, concise, and consistent.

Breakdowns in leadership often lead to communication disruptions, potentially causing decreased productivity and increased staff turnover. These breakdowns can result in reduced morale and engagement, ultimately affecting performance. A communication breakdown occurs when a message is either missed or misunderstood. Recognizing both the sender's and receiver's roles is essential. Barriers to effective communication include language differences, lack of clarity, insufficient cues, poor writing or translation, and missing details.

PERFORMANCE BREAKDOWNS

Performance breakdowns arise when set expectations for a team or organization are not met. They can result from factors such as miscommunication. Performance monitoring is essential, allowing leaders to swiftly identify and address performance hiccups, then adjust goals accordingly.

SYSTEM BREAKDOWN

It is critical for organizations to have effective processes and systems in place. Organizations with solid systems in place will garner high levels of success in effectiveness. System inconsistencies and breakdowns can impact growth, productivity, finance, and time. Any system failure or malfunction can lead to increased frustration for a leader.

It must be abundantly clear to any leader that ineffective systems make it more difficult to be successful and reach your organizational goals.

CULTURE BREAKDOWN

A culture can dictate how well an organization operates. It is essential to effectiveness and drives organizational success. A strong culture can be instrumental in shaping a successful organization. It demonstrates the leader's ability to navigate through breakdowns to enhance productivity and performance. On the other hand, an adversarial culture creates mistrust, resentment, turnovers, and incohesive systems. This type of contemptuous culture causes a leader to lose their purpose and to be off track for achieving organizational goals.

The "Be" Attitudes of Leadership

Leaders play a pivotal role in navigating these challenges. In difficult times, it's crucial for a leader to stand resilient, acknowledging that both ups and downs are part of the journey. Proactivity and a well-prepared strategy are key to overcoming such obstacles.

Leaders can fortify themselves against breakdowns by embracing the "Be" Attitudes:

Be Consistent – Be steadfast in living out your mission and accomplishing your desired goals.

Be You – Do not change who you are. Be true to yourself and your leadership style.

Be Unmovable – Do not allow anyone to railroad you out of your position. Be in it for the long haul.

Be Willing – Embrace the adversities and challenges. Consume them before they consume you.

Be a Risk Taker – Take risks! Risks involve successes and failures. Remember, you will learn and grow from your failures, so either way, you win!

Be Visible – Stay seated at every table. Know what's on the menu. If you leave the table, there is every possibility that what's on the menu may be you.

Be Focused – Stay focused on your goals. Know your directions in the dark. Keep your light shining, as difficult as it may be. Remember, a light can shine through darkness. Create a new path if necessary.

Be Transparent – Maintain clear, open, and frequent expectations and communication with all stakeholders. Remember, if you don't feed your stakeholders, they will eat you.

Be Positive – Never say "I can't do this." Remember, everything has a time and a season. Difficult days won't last forever. The darkness will pass, and light awaits you.

Be Resilient – It's okay not to be okay. Masking the pain and pretending you're okay will affect your social and emotional well-being.

Be Victorious – Find or redefine your purpose during challenging times. Don't get defeated! Remember your WHY!

Breakdowns don't always have to be a bad thing. A lot of good has developed from breakdowns in leadership. Examine yourself during the tough periods. Begin to reconnect with your whole being to shine a light on your own inner darkness.

Breakthrough!

As I entered the superintendent seat, I was faced with many breakdowns. In one organization, five principals banded together against me. They felt that one of them should have gotten the job. Many of them attempted to sabotage my leadership.

Initially, communication in meetings was marked by discord and was not received well. This small fraction of the staff had the ears of the majority of the rest of the staff. Out of 365 employees, these five individuals supervised 340 of them. This initial dysfunction caused major breakdowns in performance and communication.

This was a serious breakdown. These five employees simply intended to circumvent my leadership and report directly to the board members. A few were favorites of the board, and their strategies initially seemed to be working. I soon learned that, prior to my arrival, these individuals had been the organization's "queens" and had caused issues for previous leadership.

It was a daunting scenario. Their collective history and embedded influence made rectifying the situation more complex than a mere reprimand. A deeper strategy was required.

I recognized the need to shift the balance of power. I began by promoting two of the principals, creating an opportunity to bring fresh perspectives into the leadership team. By introducing new individuals without past affiliations, I disrupted the established group dynamics. This restructuring weakened their united front and laid the groundwork for positive change in the organization.

This was not an overnight process, but in the meantime, I had to keep a professional disposition. As such, I developed a list of attitudes to follow regardless of the breakdown. I used these "Be" Attitudes when I found myself struggling with breakdowns. These "Be" Attitudes sustained me until I was able to come up with adequate solutions.

CHAPTER 8

IF THE TRUTH HURTS

"Honesty is the first chapter in the book of wisdom." —Thomas Jefferson

Can you handle your truth? Everyone's truths are different. Sometimes we get in our own way by trying to live someone else's truths.

Leadership is hard, and a leader must step up and stand on something. That something is their truth. Even when the truth hurts, tell it anyway. Perhaps the greatest function of truth for leaders is preservation of integrity. For leaders, telling the truth is our ethical duty, and it must be taken seriously. Do not lead with lies and untruths.

A leader must build trust among all stakeholders, and you can't build trust with lies. Untruths will lead to damaged credibility. One key characteristic of a great leader is that they are able to be truthful and hold on to those truths no matter what.

The truth makes us confront hidden secrets and denials. When the truth hurts, don't run from it—acknowledge it. Telling the truth is not always a popular charge. Acknowledge that it does not sit well with others, and then face it anyway. The more you do that, the less it will hurt. Truth is not just about words but also about action. You must protect your truth through your words, actions, and deeds.

Some feel that when you deliver bad news or give critical feedback, you have to slant the truth. Somehow, telling a lie makes bad news seem more acceptable. But critical conversations must involve the absolute truth and nothing but the truth.

So many leaders steer away from having critical conversations when giving feedback. It is hard telling someone the truth about their performance.

There are lots of good reasons why the truth hurts. A colleague may be a friend, and no one likes to disappoint a friend. But organizations that embrace a truthful environment will enjoy sound organizational transformation.

Guard Your Truth

Your truth can be here today and gone tomorrow. Be who you are and what you stand for. Don't look at other leaders and what they are doing. No one is like you or is able to do what you do. Be you!

Being you means telling your truths. Own your truths and don't allow them to own you. Know and embrace who you are and what you bring to the table.

TELL YOUR TRUTH
Your truth is your superpower. It is your strength, endurance, and resilience to navigate through your leadership successfully. Allow your truth to keep you focused on your purpose. You must put aside any arrogance or pride and tell your truth.

Claim your humanity. Let constituents know what means the most to you. Claim your humanity by allowing stakeholders to see your human side. Let them know what you value and how it aligns with the organization's vision.

LIVE YOUR TRUTH
Don't live someone else's truth. Be true to who you are. All leadership experiences are different, and you must live your own experiences. You may see leaders you admire greatly and want to emulate their poise, finesse, energy, articulation, etc. Please know that you are not that leader and never will be. You will never come into yourself and your truth by trying to be someone else.

Denying your truth will hold you back from moving forward, so don't hide or suppress your truth. Truth in leadership will fulfill your life, both in and out of the leader's role. It will bring joy when joy seems far out of reach.

Stop trying to make a name for yourself. If you live your truth, your name will make you. Living your truth will allow others to see you for your authentic self. However, living your truth takes real action: connecting with your true self and becoming liberated as you move forward in leadership.

OWN YOUR TRUTH
Don't exchange the truth for a lie. One can get stuck in lies and not allow the truth to surface. As a leader, you must step into a place of ownership—owning who you are and your purpose for being a leader.

You can become comfortable with not telling the truth and with being someone you're not. This requires you to remain in the status quo and resist changes. Living in your truth is an ongoing act—it requires continual self-reflection, understanding, and the courage to grow as a leader. Owning your truth can manifest the power of self-assurance and trust in others.

COMMIT TO YOUR TRUTH

When you commit to your truth, you will follow your passion. As such, truth will define who you are and who you will become. Have a bedrock belief that you are unapologetically committed to your truth. Leaders need to stop searching for their passion. Owning your truth will lead you there.

RECLAIM YOUR TRUTH

Know that the key ingredient to your success is YOU. Have the audacity to reclaim your power.

It takes more energy to be someone you are not than to be who you were created to be. These untruths make you powerless. Raise your standards as a leader to position yourself for an evolution. Just because you are a leader does not mean you won't be afraid. It doesn't mean you won't succumb to what is popular as opposed to what is right. However, living your truth and doing what is right will take you from powerless to powerful. Leadership must be a powerful journey.

SHARE YOUR TRUTH

It's important to value the truth. This involves identifying what you hold dear while keeping in mind what is important to your stakeholders. Embrace transparency, share your beliefs, and weave them into the fabric of your leadership. This alignment between personal values and collective goals paves the way for success.

Sharing is a pivotal responsibility. Spread knowledge and strategies, and celebrate successes as they come.

In leadership, meeting the core needs of those you serve is paramount. Putting the right people in key places and sharing your truths is vital to your success. These are the people who will live these truths alongside you. You must align them with their vision of the organization. These persons can be

- staff – your core team that carries the mission forward;
- partnerships – strategic alliances that boost your objectives;
- communities – various business, political, and other societal groups that influence or get influenced by your actions;
- unions – representative bodies that voice collective concerns;
- parents – foundational stakeholders in educational or community-based endeavors;
- boards – the guiding committees that steer the direction of the organization.

RECONCILE YOUR TRUTH

To progress toward a future that resonates with your inner truths, you must exhibit resilience, particularly when confronted with trauma or adversity. Understanding the essence of reconciliation means recognizing the misalignment between one's truth and one's current situation.

Things don't have to be good in order for you to be good. But you do have to be resilient in all you do. Resilience encompasses

- looking at life through different lenses;
- having humility;
- stepping out of your comfort zones;
- staying focused and maintaining balance;

- finding value in the valueless;
- having insight and revelation.

Your personal truths will be the cornerstone of your success. These can't be found in a textbook or a seminar. Your truths may not always be popular, but you must stand up for them, even if it means you are occasionally isolated in your efforts.

Holding a leadership position does not always guarantee that others will be confident in who you are and what you hold to be truths. Stakeholders will sometimes twist your truth to suit their own beliefs. You must have the power to confront the brutal untruths.

As a leader, you may need support in confronting your truths. You may think you are not good enough and begin to supplement the truth. Know that confronting your truth will have to be an intentional action and may require employing some courageous strategies:

- Secure a mentor – A mentor can help you recognize your imperfections and inadequacies and can assist you in aligning your actions with your values.
- Have bold and courageous conversations – Don't be afraid to share your thoughts and feelings. Unleash your true self to become the leader you were called to be. Ignite that flame to become bold and productive.
- Stop pleasing others – When you stop pleasing others, you unlock your true leadership potential. Redirect the energy spent seeking external validation toward cultivating inner success.
- Awaken your understanding – Activate your self-confidence, self-worth, and self-esteem to engage in

leadership breakthroughs that will allow you to heal and redefine your leadership's purpose.
- Select self over pride every time – Don't settle for less out of desperation to validate yourself.
- Realize you have everything to lose but much more to gain – As the saying goes, you can lose the battle but still win the war. You may experience some loss, but maintain your purpose.
- Be focused and intentional – Focus on the evolution of your leadership by taking one step at a time.
- Develop a growth mindset – This will help you banish feelings of doubt and inadequacy and begin to embrace your challenges in order to change them into opportunities.

Wherever you are in your leadership journey, that is where you are supposed to be. Embrace your truths and allow your leadership the freedom to evolve.

The Truth Shall Set You Free

I survived the worst years as a leader by acknowledging and embracing my truths. I found myself at the mercy of an obstinate school board, and I faced a choice: allow their actions to define me and eventually destroy me, or choose myself and my own truths. I chose the latter.

Every leader comes to understand that the truth can be a double-edged sword—it's transformative but can also sting. Many avoid facing it, yet for leaders committed to growth and progress, embracing the truth is non-negotiable.

Within my initial days as the district's leader, my research uncovered areas of concern that I felt obligated to present to the board of education. I conducted a data presentation on student achievement scores and demonstrated the longitudinal decreases in scores over a four-year period. However, my dedication to transparency was met with denial and resistance. Board members, including some who were implicated by this data, chose to label the facts as falsehoods. I was very perplexed about how someone could think legitimate data were lies. I then realized that the board members did not want their tenure associated with poor performance, because an election was upcoming and they were on the ballot.

To me, the danger of overlooking these underperformances was palpable. I recognized the immense responsibility I held, and the truth was my guiding principle. Although the board held authority over me, compromising on my beliefs was never an option. After all, glossing over the issues would have been a disservice to the very institution we were meant to uplift.

The dilemma then arose: do I risk my professional standing for the sake of integrity? As much as I'd love to say that I was always vocal, there were moments when I chose silence over confrontation, thinking it was the safer route. Yet I soon recognized that this silence was equally damaging. Though it may have provided temporary relief, it was a burden I carried, a reminder that I wasn't living my truth fully.

In the end, my resolution was clear: I would rather face the consequences of my honesty than live a life of compromise. The truth, for me, was not just a principle but a way of life.

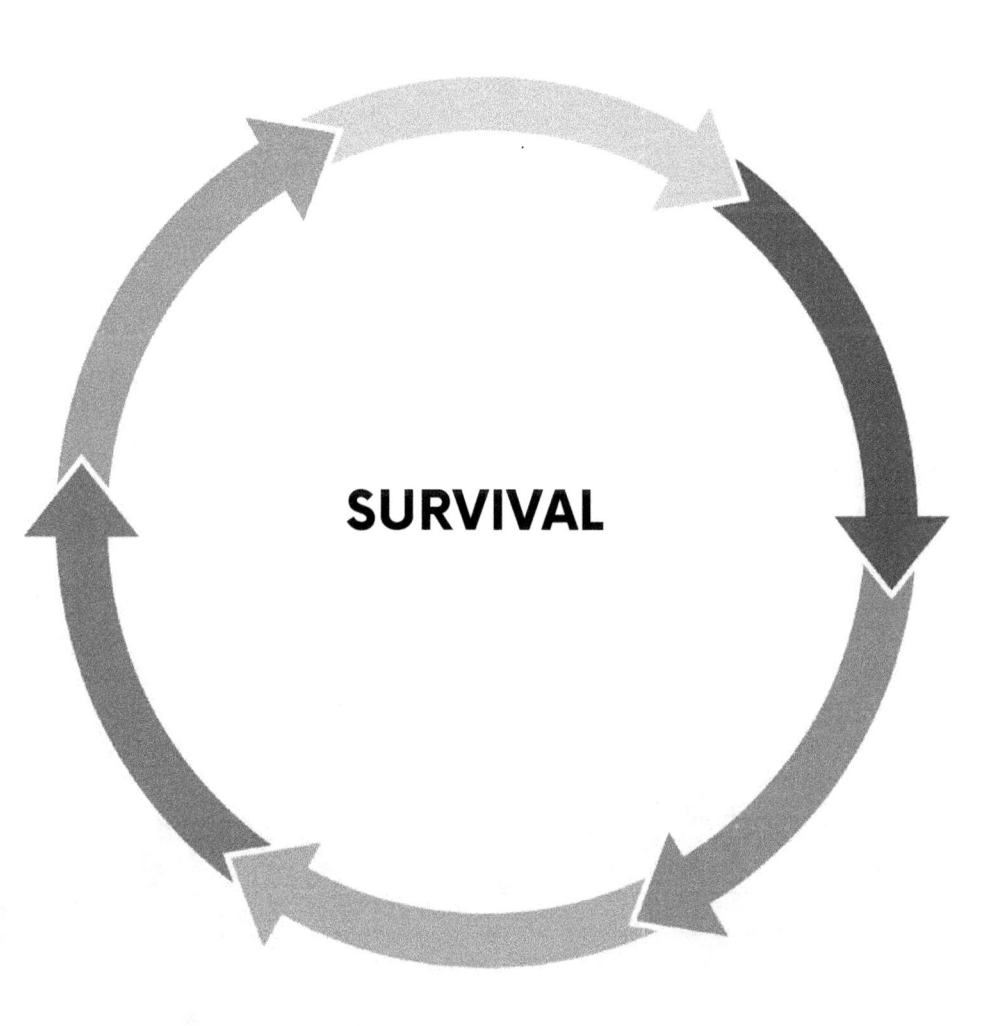

CHAPTER 9

A HILL TO DIE ON

"We cannot always choose the music life plays for us, but we can choose how we dance to it." —Unknown
"Be the most ethical, the most responsible, the most authentic you can be with every breath you take, because you are cutting a path into tomorrow that others will follow." —Ken Wilber

Leadership is a journey paved with critical decisions. A true leader consistently seeks the best possible outcomes for their organization. This journey inevitably presents battles—some worth fighting, others best avoided. It's essential to discern which is which.

Being a leader is not about occupying the top position but about sacrificing for worthy causes. No leader relishes the idea of "dying on a hill"—a metaphor for fighting a battle that may not be worth the cost. Leadership isn't about always being right. It's okay to be wrong for the right reasons.

If you die on a hill that was not worth the price, ensure that it becomes a learning experience. Occasionally, a lost battle can offer invaluable lessons. Experience, as they say, is the best teacher. The phrase "Don't die on that hill" emphasizes the importance of discernment. While leaders face battles daily, they must choose their battles wisely, considering the bigger picture.

As a leader evolves, the hills lessen, but the lessons become growth. Growing as a leader means learning which hills to climb and which to stay away from. But even tenured leaders struggle with these decisions.

When deciding what hill to die on, you as a leader must decide what is important—that is, your purpose. Battles are easier to fight when you are fighting to preserve the sanctity of your purpose. Your purpose must always drive your fight.

Every day in leadership is a battle, and you have to be aware of the battles put before you. Big or small, all hills must be assessed and approached differently.

To effectively assess whether you will die on a particular hill, you will need to take the following assessment. It's important to know the answers to the following questions before making the decision to die on a hill or move away from it:

1. Do you agree or disagree with the issue at hand? Is there a deeper issue that needs to be addressed?
2. Is the hill aligned with your leadership purpose?
3. Does the hill maintain the integrity, mission, vision, or goals of the organization?
4. From your own experiences or observations, can you determine if dying on the hill will have any impact on your overarching purpose?
5. Is this issue and its outcome worth the risk to sacrifice your purpose and move forward? Are you prepared to accept the outcome no matter which way it lands?
6. Will there be potential consequences for the outcome even if it is aligned with your leadership purpose?

7. Do you have a plan B in case the outcomes affect the progress of the organization?
8. Are you prepared for any backlash as a result of your decision?
9. Are there any areas of the issue you can adjust or revise to align with your purpose?

If the answer to most of the questions is "Yes," it is safe to say the issue aligns with your purpose, protects the organization, and is worth dying for. If the answer to most of the questions is "No," do not risk dying on the hill. As a matter of fact, get off of the hill.

Leadership is inherently complex, filled with choices that have profound impacts. Not all decisions are clear-cut, and the repercussions of certain choices can be significant. It's the duty of a leader to own their decisions, discerning carefully between battles worth fighting and those best avoided. Choosing the wrong hill to die on can be very costly.

For leaders, it's paramount to prioritize issues that drive the organization forward. The decisions that genuinely benefit the organization are those that leaders must staunchly advocate for, regardless of the outcome. Identifying these pivotal issues is essential for the overall success of an organization.

While leaders might face numerous challenges, discerning leaders recognize the vital battles and avoid unnecessary conflicts. In choosing which issues to advocate for, great leaders align their choices with the organization's mission, vision, and core values. Their decisions emanate from a place of integrity, always acting in the organization's best interest. The following are several non-negotiables that leaders should firmly stand by—hills worth dying on:

1. Mission – The organization's reason for being. This should be protected at all costs.
2. Vision – The vision of any organization should be its guide and driving force. This should always be the anchor of any organization.
3. Goals – The organizational goals must not be compromised. Never allow others to tell falsehoods that will impact the organization's goals or go against its vision.
4. Truth – Choose the truth when your leadership is in question. The truth will not let you down.
5. Integrity – There are times when your ethical values will be called into question. Stand strong and tall in your integrity.
6. Preserving the organization's products – Ensure that every decision you make is for the good of the organization, as this is what ultimately drives it forward.

No one really wants to die on a hill, but sometimes leaders will end up doing it because they did the right thing by standing for their beliefs. Sometimes hills are just worth dying on when you do it for the right reasons.

Those hills you die on can cost you, but they can also be a growth experience. Fighting for a decision you make will put you on the defensive when your decision is called into question. Making informed decisions as a leader is part of a growth journey. Knowing when to make a critical decision will emerge with experience … or after you have died on a few hills.

When leaders use their wisdom in making critical decisions, they will be more effective. They will experience enhanced growth and success. Use the prism below when you are struggling with decisions in your leadership:

Decision Prism

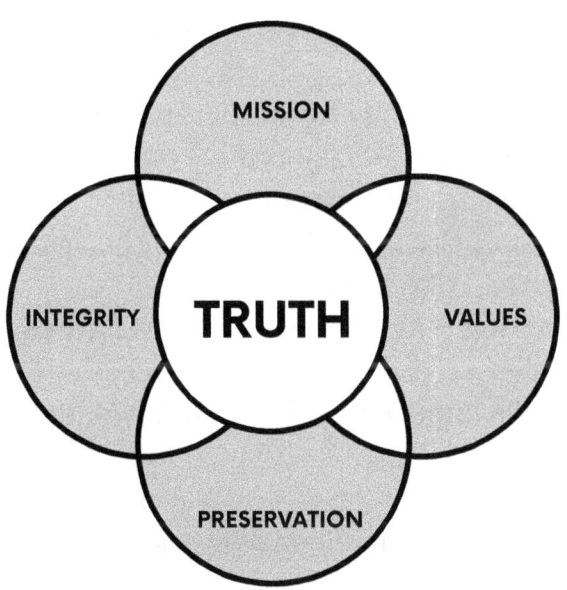

Prevention Is Key

Avoiding the land mines that will lead to wrong decisions is key to surviving the battle. This is one of the most critical elements of leadership. Avoiding them means preventing them from impeding your leadership decisions, thereby allowing you to be successful at the end of the battle (or not die on the hill). The following are areas to consider when attempting to successfully win a battle and avoid dying on a hill:

- **Clarity** – The most powerful weapon a leader can have is clear and concise communication. This helps rally the troops around a common goal.

- **Timing** – Recognizing the optimal moment to act is pivotal. It can mean the difference between victory and defeat. Strategic patience often pays dividends.
- **Research** – Properly researching or vetting an issue ensures that decisions are made based on facts and evidence. Having the facts leaves no room for mistakes. Be ready for battle. Have your ammunition.
- **Collaboration** – Collaborating with other key stakeholders makes room for healthy and unbiased decisions. Create inclusiveness. The army consists of more than one man.
- **Reflection** – Reflecting upon past battles, strengths, weaknesses, and patterns of success and failure is critically important when fighting (and winning) battles.

Do not allow personal feelings or agendas to drive you to die on a hill. Dying on a hill may have been preventable and caused by personal and negative leadership traits. Employing sound strategies and approaches will enable you to prevent wrong decisions and ultimately avoid dying on a hill.

- **Attitude** – Keep a positive attitude. Your attitude is a reflection of your character.
- **Emotions** – Control your emotions; don't let them control you or distract you from your mission.
- **Beliefs** – While deeply personal, beliefs can sometimes be misplaced. Be cautious not to project them onto others, especially when they diverge from organizational objectives.
- **Pride** – As the saying goes, "Pride comes before the fall." Be wary of letting pride cloud your judgment, pushing you to act righteously but misguidedly.

- **Impatience** – Patience is a virtue, and haste often makes waste. A patient approach ensures a clear perspective, allowing for informed decisions.
- **Power** – Power will urge you to do the wrong thing just because you can—not because it is right. The key is knowing what to do with your power. It's not about grasping onto power for its own sake but about being empowered and empowering others.
- **Distractions** – Distractions can derail your ability to be effective and hinder you from achieving your goals. Reduce distractions by keeping your purpose at the forefront and remaining steadfast in achieving your goals.

Most deaths on hills are preventable by removing personal feelings, weighing the facts, and making sound decisions when pursuing issues.

Restoring Leadership

Dying on a hill can have a devastating impact on one's leadership ability. Rebuilding will not be easy and will require much work. Depending on the severity of the loss and the reasons for dying on the hill, a leader may be required to change the landscape of their journey to bring about real transformational change within the organization.

Leadership is about accepting both the losses and the wins. After losing a battle, you must focus on how to rewind and reflect on the battle at hand, resolve issues that impeded your success, and rebuild by laying out a new plan of action. These steps will help you map out strategies for future success.

The following are the steps leaders must take after dying on a hill:

Step 1: Rewind. Stop, look, and reflect. Think about the actions you took, and connect any missing dots. Rewinding allows you to look back at the good, the bad, and the ugly parts of the battle and identify the problems. The good will be those meaningful performances that stood out and should be recognized. This could be the resiliency, tenacity, or character you and your team showed. It will be those unforgettable moments of the battle. The bad will be those visible moments when you made many mistakes or took matters personally as opposed to professionally. It can be those decisions made that were not aligned with the mission and goals of the organization. Even with the extenuating circumstances, the ugly includes the parts of the battle you may want to forget. This is where there was a breakdown in communication, timing was off, or distractions led to not being focused.

Step 2: Resolve. Analyze and evaluate the problems or issues so they can be addressed and corrected. This is where the leader uses research and data to determine the root cause of issues. Having determined the root cause, you must determine WHAT went wrong and WHY.

Step 3: Rebuild. A setback is a setup for a comeback. Chart out a renewed strategy to overcome challenges. In this rebuilding phase, transparency is paramount. Clearly outline the issues encountered and methodically plan the way forward, focusing on addressing root causes and implementing robust solutions.

Remember the age-old wisdom: "Choose your battles wisely." While not every hill is worth the sacrifice, some are. It's essential to discern this difference. When a hill isn't worth the struggle, focus on preventative strategies. Keep personal emotions at bay, but always march forward with a well-thought-out strategy for success.

No Time to Die

One of the greatest lessons I have learned as a leader is the importance of discerning which hills are not worth dying on.

I personally died on many hills during my first years as a school superintendent. I attempted to defend every decision I made. It felt as if every query was an affront to my leadership, even though I was still finding my footing in the role and grappling with pivotal decisions.

A particular point of contention was the manner in which the board sought information from me. Their approach felt overzealous, and I was keen to communicate my reservations. Over dinner, a seasoned colleague offered insights that would reshape my leadership approach. "Choose the hills you're willing to die on," she advised. She highlighted my tendency to take matters too personally, allowing emotions to overshadow logic. She urged me to pause, reflect, and strategize before diving into battles. Her defining words of wisdom were "If the battle isn't about what's best for the children, it's not worth it."

Heeding her counsel, I anchored my decisions and battles around core principles: vision, goal, truth, integrity, and always the best interests of the children. To help navigate these choices, I devised a T-chart delineating what was worth fighting for and what wasn't. This simple tool steered me through many a leadership challenge, ensuring I expended energy where it truly mattered.

Hills to Die On	Hills Not to Die On
Mission	Attitude
Vision	Emotions
Goals	Belief
Truth	Pride
Integrity	Power
Preserving the organization's products	Distractions

CHAPTER 10

FIT TO BE TIED

"I survived because the fire inside of me burned brighter than the fire around me." —Joshua Graham

Survival of the Fittest

Your leadership is not an accident. Everyone has some type of leadership within them, whether they want to be a leader or not. A leader must know and love what they do. They must also be disciplined about that love. Being disciplined holds a promise of what is to come and gives a direction for what is. Exercising discipline without direction is drudgery.

Leaders must have tough skin. A thick skin allows a leader to roll with the punches, confronting obstacles head-on and devising strategies for those they can't directly overcome. This leader has the ability to withstand criticism and insults—which will come when you are not liked, or when you make an unpopular decision. This leader is always ready and willing to combat adversity.

A thick skin does not mean you are emotionless. You will still feel the pain of leadership; you are just emotionally fit to handle it. Thick-skinned leaders are not closed-minded; they are open to feedback that will allow them to improve upon their leadership skills. If your skin is thick, you will be protected from the extreme heat of the fire. Thick skin doesn't just appear; you must be intentional in developing it to survive your leadership experience. You can be intentional in the following ways:

MOVE THE GOALPOSTS—ESTABLISH HIGHER STANDARDS

Being successful in leadership requires you to choose to be different – Moving the goalposts. Shifting the goalposts in leadership can hold a positive or negative connotation. However, shifting one's standards for the better can be a positive direction for a leader.

Raising your standards will allow you to lead by example while motivating and inspiring others to strive for greatness. Raising your standards will also lead to being trusted by your team and foster a positive and productive environment.

Moving the goalposts also entails remaining focused on the end goal of the organization. Moving the goalposts also entails remaining focused on the end goal of the organization and standing strong in your actions:

- Do not lower your standards to please others. Lowering your standards can lead to lack of confidence in one's self and ability. Keeping your standards high will increase confidence in yourself and the trust of others.
- Do not engage in any unethical practices.
- Do not compromise your values. There are huge consequences for compromising your values; your leadership will no longer be trustworthy in your eyes or the eyes of others.
- Do not sugarcoat reality. Do not pretend. Know and accept where you are so you can adjust and plan for where you are going.

USE YOUR OWN RULER

The fuel for being fit for the job comes from fixing your sight on the goal. You cannot do the job on cruise control. You are either on the gas or on the brakes. The question becomes: If I am on the gas, how fast am I going? How do I determine if I am moving too fast or too slow? You have to use your own ruler to measure based on your current situation.

MANAGE INSECURITIES

Every leader has their own unique mission. Leadership is a huge commitment, and you have to go into it with your eyes open. You will struggle with many insecurities. You must manage those insecurities and not let them weigh down your thinking. Use them as guiding posts to measure your growth. These insecurities can be physical, mental, or emotional, and they may involve numerous topics, such as

- being accepted by stakeholders and the business and political communities;
- meeting goals;
- knowing everything;
- pleasing everyone.

You must manage your insecurities, or they will manage you. You can accomplish this by digging down and facing the different aspects of your insecurities:

- Fears – What fears are holding you back from making bold choices? Be intentional about what to do.
- Reasons for not meeting your goals – Learn why you may not be meeting your goals and what you do and do not do. What can you do differently?

- Need to please – You can never please everyone. Trying to please everyone will cause unnecessary stress.
- Need to know – Nourish yourself with knowledge. Learn all you can and be a continual learner.

DO NOT TAKE SHORTCUTS

Shortcuts can impede your leadership trajectory. Have a plan; know what direction you are going, and know the speed limits. This plan allows you to focus on the main things and not veer off into unknown territories.

GET OUT OF YOUR OWN WAY

Don't get in your way … find your way. Stay focused on your goals. Put aside your ego or anything that will hold you back from reaching your greatest potential. Don't be self-centered or have self-doubt; instead, gain self-confidence by learning to explore compromise, positivity, and creativity.

MESS OR MESSAGE?

A leader must be heard and understood through their messages. Messaging allows leaders to develop a connection between themselves and their workforce. When giving the wrong message, a leader will eliminate workplace chatter, dissatisfaction and misunderstandings. As such, giving the right message will lead to trust, productivity, and connections.

A leader must be confident in their message. Getting the right message out entails
- developing reliable communication protocols;
- knowing your audience – tailor the message to the right audience;
- having a purpose – focus and align the information with ideas and goals;

- being clear and concise – ensure accurate transmission of information;
- giving the facts – conduct proper research and homework;
- being respectful – be mindful of tone, facial expressions, gestures, etc.

The right sentence can come in verbal or written form. Either way, one can transmit valuable information effectively. Some leaders may prefer one form over the other. In verbal messaging, leaders can relay ideas using more facial and body expressions and word tones. However, in written messaging, the leader can be more detailed and concise.

STAY WOKE!
Never sleep behind the wheel. It is when you are sleepy while driving the organization that accidents and fatalities occur. Leadership calls for constant focus. Be alert to anything that poses a threat to your administration. The minute you fall asleep behind the leadership wheel, you fall prey to others:

- boards
- staff
- community
- stakeholders
- political interests

Sleep places you in a state of illusion, and you will be susceptible to false assumptions. Don't get sidetracked. Don't allow others to take you off course. Don't allow yourself and your ego to cloud your view. The power is not in your title but in the journey. You cannot enjoy the ride or reach your destination if you are asleep.

I Choose Survival

The COVID-19 pandemic was a major crisis, but it was only one of the many crises I experienced throughout my leadership. Not every crisis spells doom; some usher in transformative opportunities. These moments spotlighted vulnerabilities in our organizational culture.

Regarding embracing change: Many times, my board made decisions that I did not agree with. However, being the leader of the organization and under the auspices of the board, I was faced with conceding if the decisions did not violate my personal "Hill to Die On" policy. At times, to work alongside a board of directors, I had to accept their ideas and suggestions for the organization. I had to keep in mind that I was a team member. Therefore, for better or worse, it was my duty to ensure that their decisions were considered, even though they sometimes did not match the goal of the organization. I had to work with managers who embraced new ideas and new directions. Without letting go of my purpose, I occasionally had to manage situations I was strongly against. I found myself faced with challenges that were threatening my survival and, as a result, the survival of the organization.

My survival was typically incumbent upon how I addressed the issues and responded to the many challenges. Despite my feelings and thoughts, I still had to strengthen and sustain a culture in the midst of a crisis. I had to navigate these difficult times while continuing to proceed with dignity and respect. When my resolve wavered, I had to remove my personal feelings and consider the organizational goals.

A crisis will bring about many insecurities. To manage my insecurities, I had to quickly sharpen my knowledge. Leaders are not perfect people. I had to recognize and accept my insecurities before I could manage them. The many crises I encountered allowed my superpowers to surface.

I attribute my survival and success to having thick skin and keeping survival strategies on hand to help me focus. These strategies did not emerge overnight but were developed as I struggled through many crises:

1. Sharpen your knowledge – Measure with your own ruler.
2. Uphold dignity and respect – Turn your mess into your message.
3. Remove personal feelings – Stay woke. Don't take it personally.
4. Validate your purpose – Maintain a purpose.
5. Be resilient – Take no shortcuts.
6. Ignite change – Move the goalpost. Step out of your comfort zone.
7. Value the journey – Stay in the driver's seat and drive your own car.
8. Acknowledge and manage insecurities – As knowledge grows, insecurities decrease.
9. Laugh often – Get out of your own way. Have fun! Laugh to keep from crying.
10. Embrace positivity – Locate the positive and keep it close, or the negativity will overcome it.

These principles not only anchored me during turbulent phases but also illuminated the way, ensuring that the organization's purpose and objectives remained clear and attainable.

Be in the Know

Attaining the top seat is only half of the battle. Sitting in the top seat can be extremely challenging, as well as stressful. The position can take a physical and psychological toll on you. Whether you have been with the company for many years and worked your way to the top or you are new to the organization, learning to survive the top is key.

KNOW OTHERS

The top seat can be lonely, because you are the only one in the organization with the top title. Loneliness can be attributed to a lack of confidence in others, but it is actually a lack of confidence in oneself that can lead one to work without support or guidance. While the apex of leadership might seem singular—after all, there's typically one "top" position in an organization—it doesn't necessitate isolation. There's a misconception among some leaders that they must shoulder the weight alone, especially if they have unparalleled titles or responsibilities. This mindset, while seemingly showcasing strength, can impede a leader's growth, ushering in feelings of isolation.

By contrast, true leadership recognizes the value of collaboration. Success isn't a solitary journey. Leaders benefit immensely from aligning with peers and professionals in similar leadership spheres. Such connections offer more than just camaraderie; they present opportunities for personal and professional growth. Collaborative endeavors, be it seeking guidance on critical decisions or sharing experiences, amplify a leader's capacity to achieve their objectives.

Support in leadership is the bedrock of enhanced confidence, continuous learning, and the tenacity to navigate the myriad challenges that come with the role. For holistic development, leaders not only must be proactive in extending support but also should be open to receiving it. Nurturing reciprocal relationships with peers can amplify a leader's efficacy and professionalism.

After all, how can someone truly inspire and motivate if they themselves remain untouched by motivation or inspiration? Leadership is as much about imparting wisdom and guidance as it is about learning and being guided. To lead is to be in a constant dance of giving and receiving support.

KNOW YOUR BLIND SPOTS

Survival in leadership entails finding your blind spots. Your leadership blind spots are areas where your view will be obstructed. These are sensitive areas that are important to success.

Sometimes these are areas in which a leader fails to use good discernment. Your blind spot can be a person, a policy, a budget, etc. that is preventing you from moving forward. Blind spots can impede productivity, limit organizational growth, and prevent a leader from ultimately being successful. Blind spots are those invisible chains that prevent leaders from being their best.

Being aware of leadership blind spots is also about being aware of oneself. A blind spot can be difficult to detect if a leader is overconfident, prideful, power-driven, or authoritative. In other areas, these attributes have their place. However, when you are in the top leadership role, it is essential to be able to see the entire picture of the organization.

KNOW YOURSELF

If a leader has a leadership style that is having an adverse effect on the growth of the organization, this could mean a change in style is needed. A leader must be aware of how their leadership style is affecting the organization. Great leaders have high levels of self-awareness, whether intentionally or not.

If self-awareness is not innate, a leader must create an intentional process by which they pursue it. This will promote a better perspective on their leadership. Self-awareness activities can include journaling, ongoing self-reflecting, reconnecting with staff and programs, setting check-in schedules, paying attention to details, and asking many questions.

Self-awareness is essential to survival as a leader. Self-aware leaders must know themselves and have the ability to evaluate themselves and the situations they are placed in. They must stay aware of their feelings, actions, and thoughts to make better decisions when directing the organization.

Self-awareness in leadership will do the following:

- decrease stress
- promote better decision-making
- build self-confidence
- provide motivation
- enhance communication with stakeholders
- build relationships with stakeholders
- control thoughts and emotions
- enhance organizational outcomes

Becoming aware of oneself can lead to improved decision-making. Leaders can see their own views, as well as the views of others, as important. Self-aware leaders adjust their leadership style and are more likely to have leadership longevity.

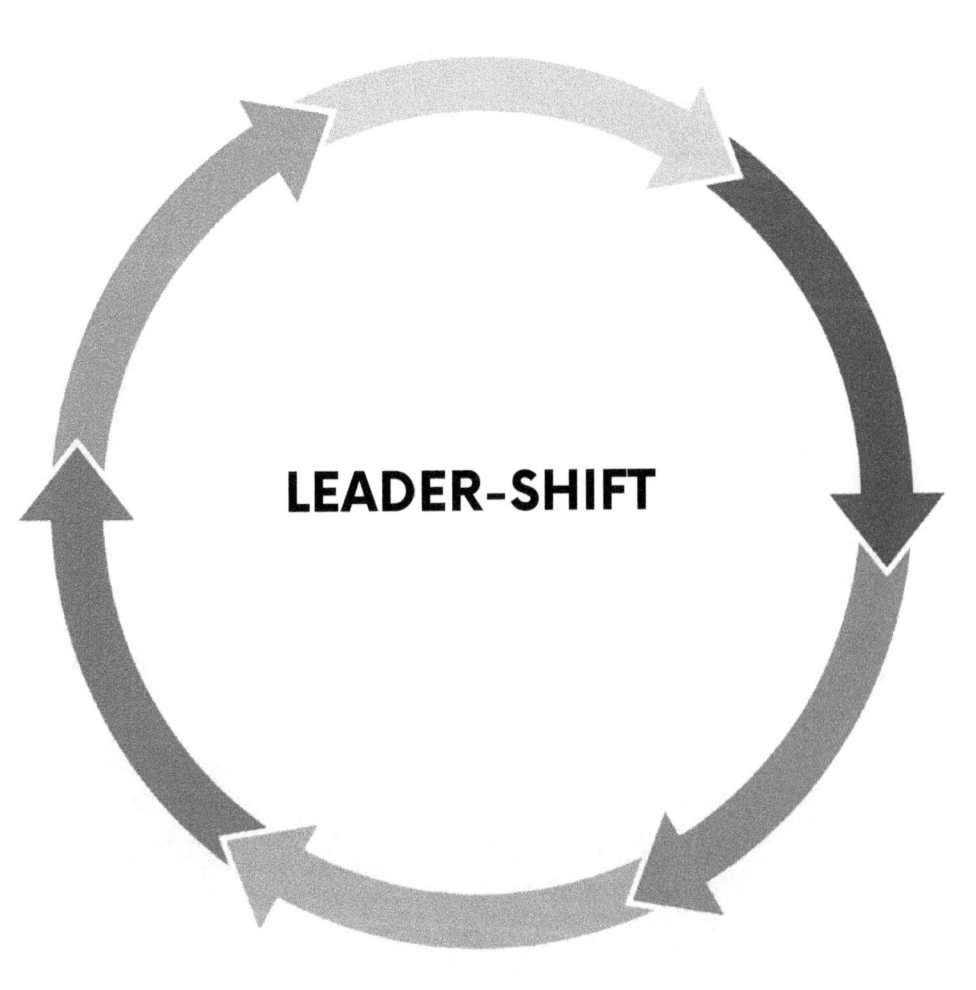

CHAPTER 11

CONSIDER A SHIFT – DON'T STAY TOO LONG

"Leader-shift is the ability and willingness to make a leadership change that will positively enhance organizational and personal growth." —John Maxwell

When it comes to leadership, many institutions have a revolving door. It is an ongoing battle with internal and external enemies. It's critical to consider where your position will lead you. As leaders evolve, they make significant shifts in their leadership. These shifts serve to fulfill their mission as a leader. Leaders must continue to measure their effectiveness throughout their service. When you are no longer successful, it's time for a leader-shift. You must make decisions to shift your leadership within or outside the organization. This leader-shift represents a conscious decision to adjust one's leadership approach, whether that means transforming within the current organization or transitioning to a new one. Embracing this shift isn't merely about changing direction; it's about seeing situations and events with renewed clarity and purpose. If you are going to continue on the path of leadership, you must make a shift that will create your own path to success.

Leadership must be a life of clarification, not confusion. A leader-shift will release you from mental and emotional stress and help you find peace in your leadership. It will help you transition to a new leadership roadmap. You might be paralyzed by your leadership, but a leader-shift will help you maintain balance and perspective.

Moreover, a leader-shift isn't just a reactive measure; it's proactive. It enables leaders to channel their accumulated knowledge and experiences into novel strategies or ventures. This could manifest as a different role, a new career avenue, or even a transition into retirement. Regardless of the specifics, a leader-shift isn't about conceding defeat. Instead, it symbolizes an empowered choice to evolve, free from the anxieties that often cloud leadership.

You will know when it's time to make a shift. This revelation may come over time, or it could hit you like a stack of bricks. There are many reasons you might find yourself ready for a leader-shift:

YOUR A-LIST STATUS CHANGES TO F-LIST
A-list leadership is a status all leaders strive for in this position of power. It is the top status, and you're most likely to enjoy it during the honeymoon phase or the early stages of your leadership. This is when leadership is good and the leader is able to make a difference. It is during this period that the leader enjoys the job. They are leveraging their influence to improve organizational processes. Communication is clear, problems are limited, and the leader is supported by their governing teams or boards. However, when the A becomes an F, for whatever reason, and the rift is irreconcilable, think about a shift.

YOUR VOICE IS MUTED BY GOVERNANCE
As a leader, you are communicating across the organization to a board of trustees, vendors, employees, and stakeholders every day. Your voice is the key that will enable you to convey

a successful message. Try reclaiming your voice to take back your power. Communicate your vision and core values. Finding your voice helps to strengthen your confidence and others' perceptions of you. Reclaiming your voice can require expanding your circle of influence, changing your message, and elevating your words to inspire change. When your voice becomes muted, think about a shift.

YOUR LEADERSHIP IS DOMINATED BY NEGATIVITY
Negativity has a domino effect in the workplace when leadership is undervalued and over-criticized by others. The leader's interactions are impacted and morale is derailed by the negativity. If you can no longer find any good and are unable to transform negativity into positivity, it's time for a shift.

YOUR WORK ENVIRONMENT BECOMES TOXIC
Sometimes, a leader enjoys a great work environment that is well suited to and aligned with their vision. However, in a blink of an eye, that environment can transition into one that is extremely toxic. Toxic leadership can have an adverse effect on the leader and on the organization. Toxic leadership will lead to low morale, poor communication, and low productivity. This behavior will destroy the culture and climate of the organization. Sometimes leaders are unaware of their toxicity, and the only way past it is to make a shift.

YOU FEEL IMPRISONED BY YOUR ROLE
The top seats are most leader's dream jobs; this is what they have worked for throughout most of their careers. They climbed the career ladder and finally made it to the top. These jobs are the pinnacle of their career, and they're making the most money they've ever made in their lives. But the dream job can become a nightmare when a leader feels trapped in the top position.

A leader must be free to learn, grow, and produce for the well-being of the organization. When you are trapped or stunted professionally, or when you are no longer relevant and your leadership comes with conditions that are not aligned with your vision, consider a shift.

THE BAD CIRCUMSTANCES OUTWEIGH THE GOOD

Leadership is about leveraging the good with the bad. *The bad in leadership is always stronger than the good.* When leadership gives you lemons, don't just make lemonade; make decisions for self-preservation and for the good of the organization you lead. Such decisions may involve a shift in direction.

YOUR PHYSICAL AND MENTAL WELL-BEING ARE IN JEOPARDY

A leader must protect their own mental wellness. As a leader, you cannot effectively lead if you are physically and emotionally drained. Leaders must recognize the impact their position can have on their overall physical and mental health.

One of the most difficult things to do is make decisions based on our mental well-being—especially when it comes to major decisions that will shift our long-term trajectory. Leaders want to feel like they have it all together and tend to overlook the signs of mental malfunction. Despite all obstacles, many tend to stay in these jobs when their mental well-being is at stake.

Some might judge it unwise to leave the top role, but doing so can have a positive impact on your social and emotional well-being and, ultimately, on your future. Your leadership must be energized daily if you are going to survive in the role. That energy helps leaders remain dedicated to and passionate about their role.

YOUR PASSION ESCAPES YOU
Surviving without passion is dead leadership and a call for action. If you are no longer passionate about your role, it doesn't mean you're incapable of performing it well. It simply means it may be time for a change. It could mean that your passion can be fulfilled somewhere else. Maybe you never even had a passion for the role, but you inherited it because you were seen as the ideal internal candidate. This is not uncommon and often results in a passionless leader.

According to research, the longevity of most top leadership roles averages between three and a half and four and a half years. However, some successful leaders lead organizations for far longer. The question is, Are they still passionate? If so, how do they keep their passion ignited for so long? Passion is the driving force for successful leaders, and when it leaves, so should the leader. Leaders can reignite their passion or decide that it is time to change the game.

In Pursuit of Sanity

Time is ever present in our lives. Nevertheless, many of us wish we had more of it—more time to lead the perfect department, system, or organization. The reality is, we will forever chase time. This means we will often sacrifice personal time and space. Unfortunately, for leaders, this typically means sacrificing the time we would normally spend with family, socializing, or relaxing.

As a leader, you're often inundated with many tasks, many people, and many responsibilities. Leaders often find themselves on a never-ending treadmill, chasing the pressures of managing staff, balancing budgets, overseeing numerous departments, and meeting deadlines. The pressure to constantly be at 100% is heightened daily. The reality of being a practicing leader is that you are always on that never-ending treadmill, with no end in sight.

To remain sane, a leader must look at their leadership as a positive movement. Your labor will birth new life for those coming after you. But you must first turn off the treadmill. Select self-worth over net worth. Your self-worth should win over money every time. Be thankful for the opportunity, but move on. Let the experiences you've gained direct you to a new path.

LEADERSHIP STRESSORS

Stress and pressure resulting from leadership is not uncommon; actually, it's commonplace. These stressors can impact your personal and professional lives if they are not controlled. They can also affect your mental health and well-being. When your leadership is not fulfilling you personally or professionally, or is causing you mental stress, it may be time to plan a strategic exit. Exiting could take the form of stepping down, leaving the organization, or retiring.

Unfortunately, most leaders will experience leadership stress. It can surface early or late in the leadership journey. Leadership stress, like any stress, can become harmful to your health. Many things can lead to stress in leadership, and it is important to recognize when these stressors surface.

Often, a leader chalks stress up to being overwhelmed or tired when, in essence, it's way more than that. Stress is a silent attacker and can cause great harm if it is not addressed. Addressing it entails moving away from the cause of the stress.

Stress can prevent leaders from achieving success. The effects of stress are sometimes hidden, such as silent health challenges. Only a change can relieve the stress—whether that's a change in the dynamics of the job or a change of job. Changing the dynamics of the job can involve changing a system, changing legislation, or changing policy—three things you often do not have the power to change.

But a leader can put a stressful task in perspective by not only relieving stress in the moment but also deciding when and how to eliminate it.

Remember that deciding to leave a leadership role is not a failure. It just means making a change in your current circumstances for health reasons.

CONSIDER A CHANGE

If you are no longer excited about your role or it is no longer satisfying, it is time to exit. You can exit and move into another leadership role without loss of salary or dignity. You can also consider transitioning to another field of interest. When considering a change, remember the following:

1. Don't stay too long – If not now, when?
2. Plan an exit – Create an exit plan to ensure a sound transfer of duties.
3. Don't wear out your welcome – Do not extend your stay when your time is up!
4. Heed the writing on the wall:
   - See the signs.
   - Don't wait for it to get better, because it won't.
   - Trust your judgment.
   - Follow your heart.

5. History will get in the way of destiny – Move on!
6. When you're done, be unapologetic for the journey. No regrets!

You may have waited many years to get into a leadership position, but know that all good things must come to an end.

There is no such thing as perfect leadership. The journey may not be all that you imagined it to be. Perhaps the job is just not meeting your needs. It can go from sweet to bitter at any time. The key is knowing when it is time to move on.

Sometimes you can outgrow your role. Your passion could be fading, or things are just not what they used to be. Know that staying will not benefit you or the organization. There is more out there awaiting you; just know when it's time to make a change.

Leadership is a unique journey not meant for everyone. Recognizing when to pivot or adjust your approach is essential. True leadership resonates deep within, moving beyond a position to a sense of purpose. While leading might be part of your journey, it doesn't necessarily define your destination. It's completely acceptable to find that a primary leadership role isn't the right fit for you. In such cases, free yourself from that weight and seek your genuine place. Sometimes, your most impactful role may not be as the top leader but as a key support or strategist. If you're contemplating a shift, consider the following insights:

- When it does not feel right … it's not!
- When the vitality of your leadership is compromised … it's time to leave.
- When your primary reasons for accepting the role become secondary … it's time to leave.

- When your service becomes slavery ... it's time to leave!
- When your negatives outweigh your positives ... it's time to leave!
- When your professionalism is compromised ... it's time to leave!
- When your vision gets cloudy ... it's time to leave!

Leadership can be a painful path, but there is joy awaiting you out there. You can only obtain that joy after you leave a situation where you are stagnated.

DON'T WEAR OUT YOUR WELCOME

The challenges you face within the course of your leadership will redefine who you are as a leader and help you make some life-changing decisions. Do not stay too long in a role that you are not, or can no longer be, successful in or that you are no longer welcome in. Know when it's time to make your exit and plan it accordingly. Don't hesitate to exit, or it will be a bumpy ride. If your leadership is not working and there are external and internal forces preventing you from fixing your broken leadership, you should plan your exit. Plan your exit by asking yourself the following **What Ifs:**

- What if you are not able to fix a broken leadership?
- What if your leadership journey is in the hands of others?
- What if the leadership role is no longer fun?
- What if your leadership is causing you trauma?
- What if you are being managed by outside forces (a board, trustees, etc.)?
- What if you know your leadership has hit a dead end?

- What if you believe you have no more skin in the game?
- What if you are losing sight of your humanity?
- What if you are no longer valued?
- What if you are losing sight of reality?
- What if you are no longer honored and respected?
- What if your purpose is no longer fulfilled?

When the Writing Is on the Wall

When the writing on the wall states that your time in a leadership role has come to an end, you must make a leader-shift. Sometimes, leader-shifting will help deliver you from forced or unwarranted situations.

"Writing on the wall" is an idiom that means a sign of imminent doom—that something negative will be happening soon. Seeing the writing on the wall allows leaders to know when to leave on their own terms, before being forced to leave. Your now does not have to be your always. You must move away from the role and redefine your purpose when all of the signs of doom are visible and clear.

If your walls could talk, what would they say?

- Leave by any means necessary
- Timing is everything
- Time's up
- Renew your leadership
- Accept the inevitable
- You've reached the end
- No time for personal history
- Take your place
- It's time for a transition
- The curtains are closed
- The time has come
- Peace that changes the past
- Shift now
- Your destiny awaits you
- Longevity has its place and time

Your destiny is more decipherable than you realize. You just have to heed the messages on the wall. These messages should unleash your history and let the chains fall off.

History vs. Destiny

The journey of leadership often requires significant dedication and effort. Yet getting anchored in past achievements or setbacks can hinder progression. While one's history can provide valuable insights, being overly fixated on it might lead the leader into uncharted territories. When wielded wisely, the past can serve as a beacon, guiding one's future direction in a positive manner.

History can be full of both negatives and positives. But when the negatives clearly outweigh the positives, you must steer away from history. Those negative things can be failures, setbacks, breakdowns, deficits, discouragements, etc.

When you return to a dark place in the history of your leadership, you will find yourself confused and lost. Find a light at the end of the tunnel. That light will be your way out of history and into a vibrant future. Release the past so you can embrace a new future.

Don't be confused in deciding when to let go. Don't question whether to hold on to history or move forward. Great leaders learn to place a period where others put a question mark. Allow your destiny to outweigh history and bring a story to its end. Great leaders keep moving forward so they can walk into their new destiny.

Be intentional about claiming your destiny. Your destiny is your new direction ... be ready to claim it!

Changing the Game

While changing the game in leadership might seem a little daunting, there comes a time to think about a much-needed professional transition. When circumstances change, you must consider realigning those personal considerations before making that move.

Analyze your current situation. Taking a good look at where you are currently can help you determine the magnitude of changes you will need to execute. You may have outgrown your current role and be looking for a new challenge or opportunity to pursue your goals.

Such transitions can either be methodically mapped out or occur suddenly. Regardless, change is a given. If your present role isn't in harmony with your envisioned future, feelings of stagnation might emerge. It's only natural to seek richer prospects.

Change is inevitable and can make a difference in your leadership progression. Whether you are changing employers or moving into a completely different profession, it takes a well-aligned strategy to be successful. Change is always a daunting prospect, especially in our careers. But learning how to realign your leadership in the midst of adversities will help your professional transition be a more sound process.

Implementing a leadership change is not easy and will take a lot of work. The following framework will help leaders navigate through the change process for a sound professional transition. These steps cover the entire process of transitioning your leadership.

People change careers at all stages of their career journey and for a range of reasons, from wanting a more flexible schedule and the ability to work from anywhere to craving new challenges and more fulfillment. Professional change will require some effort, but the payoff can be life-changing.

No matter where the professional transition leads you, it's important to navigate it carefully. Below is a detailed list of steps that can help you feel confident as you develop a plan and drive the change process.

There are seven key activities to rely on as you consider a professional transition:

R – Reflect, Recognize, Reject, Restore, Release

E – Examine, Evaluate, Embrace, Expect, Employ

A – Analyze, Accept, Alter, Affirm, Accelerate

L – Look, Leap, Learn, Launch, Liberate

I – Investigate, Inventory, Identify, Ignite, Inspire

G – Gauge, Gain, Guard, Generate, Gravitate

N – Number, Note, Navigate, Never

Let's look at this list in more detail:

R	**Reflect, Recognize, Reject, Restore, Release**
	Reflect on your journey and all you've experienced.
	Recognize the reality that it is over.
	Reject complacency.
	Restore your integrity to maintain your self-assurance.
	Release any void and prepare for lifestyle and work-life changes.

E	**Examine, Evaluate, Embrace, Expect, Employ**
	Examine your self-worth and realize your value.
	Evaluate your motives and reasoning.
	Embrace the unknowns of the change to come.
	Expect the best, but be prepared for the worst.
	Employ a new direction that will lead to change.

A	**Analyze, Accept, Alter, Affirm, Accelerate**
	Analyze the facts and draw some conclusions.
	Accept the inevitable and face reality of restoration.
	Alter your thoughts and actions.
	Affirm that change is needed by looking at the facts.
	Accelerate your plan of action.

L	**Look, Leap, Learn, Launch, Liberate**
	Look for the land mines you may encounter in your pursuit.
	Leap forward toward new goals and opportunities.
	Learn from your experiences to fill any voids.
	Launch a plan of action in pursuit of your destiny.
	Liberate your soul by living with the freedom of knowing.

I	**Investigate, Inventory, Identify, Ignite, Inspire**

Investigate next steps to confront change and navigate your transition journey.

Inventory your circumstances and have the courage to face reality.

Identify a path forward and become obsessed with change.

Ignite change by setting a target date for transitioning.

Inspire change by preparing yourself to let go.

G	**Gauge, Gain, Guard, Generate, Gravitate**

Gauge your mindset. Be determined to be bold and courageous in your pursuit of change.

Gain wisdom from knowing you have done all that is within your purview.

Guard your integrity so you can preserve and restore yourself through the transition.

Generate a plan for transitioning from the known to the unknown.

Gravitate toward the exit. Throw out the anchor to stop the ship.

N	**Number, Note, Navigate, Never**

Number the days and execute your plan to move forward.

Note your value and accomplishments to be comfortable in your new skin.

Navigate the impending separation and walk into your destiny. Be well pleased with your successes and challenges.

Never look back. Avoid flashbacks and setbacks, and only focus on the comeback.

Remember, leadership is forever evolving. Transitioning into a new career or a new line or level of work will happen to both the worst and the best of leaders. To consistently REALIGN your transitional approaches, you can get up and realize that change is inevitable, get out of your current situation, and get on to a new, more suitable endeavor.

It may take years to cultivate and perfect leadership or to reach one's peak. It about the lessons you learn throughout your leadership journey. Make sure you learn from your failures, mistakes, trials, and errors. Every leader has their moment in the sun, and inevitably, seasons shift. However, a change in season doesn't signify a conclusion. Leadership is marked by beginnings and endings, and recognizing the right moment to transition is crucial. When the signs align, it's an invitation to ascend to greater heights.

You can't have a new season in life until you release the old season. Do not hold on to an old season; know when to let go. This does not mean there is nothing next. Letting go could simply mean evolving. Walk through another revolving door—the open door will allow you to see your way to your next journey ... or back to the top.

After This

A bizarre and somewhat disturbing feeling happened to me near the end of my tenure, following a very tumultuous board meeting where the board and I saw very different perspectives. This encounter demonstrated to me that my time was up. A voice came to me and shared that I had reached the end. At that point, I knew I had to make a leader-shift. I needed to redefine my leadership purpose.

The writing was on the wall! The phrase "the writing is on the wall" is often used to describe an impending disaster. In this case, it denoted that a state of doom was about to fall upon me as a leader or the organization I was leading.

It was vital for me to first see the writing and then interpret and explain the meaning of the message. The meaning of the writing on the wall became visible quickly. I attempted to make my own interpretations, but these enigmatic words had me puzzled. The writing on the wall was getting larger and clearer as time went on. As I came to read the handwriting on the wall and translate it to my situation, I quickly began to make some shifts in my leadership.

I was finally accepting the fact that the board and I were headed in different directions. We no longer shared the same vision, and trust on both ends was lost. With this in mind, it was made clear to me that it made no tactical sense for me to remain in a role in which my voice and talents were suppressed.

Initially, I engaged in a mind fight. I began to tell myself I needed more years to build upon my legacy. I had plans to build two new structures. But even though I had an abundance of plans to build the organization to great heights, the writing was there for me.

My decision to shift became jarring for me. At first glance, it seems as though I got unreasonably angry at myself for thinking about walking away from everything I had built. But I came to realize the ignorance and audacity of my thoughts.

I had to stay vigilant that the members of my board were who they were and I had no control over their actions. However, I did have control over my own actions and pathways.

I then began to focus my attention on protecting my well-being. My leadership was no longer valued, and change was inevitable. It was up to me to repair a broken situation and realign my goals for moving forward.

I saw the writing on the wall, and I became prepared by first asking myself: What if I was no longer in the top seat? Did I want to secure a new leadership role? What did I desire to do outside of occupying the top seat? What would keep me relevant? Where did I need to be to maintain my financial goals?

I realigned my thoughts and actions and made a decision to leave the organization at the close of my contract.

Whatever my next move was going to be, I planned to take full advantage of the six years in the top seat and the lessons learned as I prepared for life after that leadership role. I'm grateful for the strategies developed and lessons learned during my top leadership experience and have intentionally and professionally moved on and out with dignity. There is life after any leadership experience.

Recognizing that we are constantly evolving and that change is inevitable is half of the battle in a leader's journey. It's essential for leaders to distinguish between the concepts of evolution and change, even as they intersect. Leadership is a cycle of evolution that must either engage in or end in a leader-shift.

Now that you have read this book, it is my hope that you will be able to thrive as a leader using the many strategies presented here.

When one's leadership evolves through the phases, the cycle can continue evolving or it can end, at which point a new cycle is free to begin.

Leadership is forever evolving.

REFERENCES

Brown, Brené. *Dare to Lead: Brave Work. Tough Conversations. Whole Hearts.* Random House. 2018.

Charan, Ram. *The High Potential Leader: How to Grow Fast, Take on New Responsibilities, and Make an Impact.* Wiley & Sons, 2017.

Collins, Jim. *From Good to Great: Why Some Companies Make the Leap and Others Don't.* HarperBusiness, 2001.

Drucker, Peter F. *On Leadership.* Harvard Business School Publishing, 2011.

Dungy, Tony. *The Mentor Leader: Secrets to Building People and Teams That Win Consistently.* Tyndale House, audiobook, 2015.

Friedman, Edwin H. *A Failure of Nerve: Leadership in the Age of the Quick Fix.* rev. ed. Church Publishing, 2017.

Glanz, Jeffrey. *Finding Your Leadership Style: A Guide for Educators.* ASCD, 2002.

Goleman, Daniel, Richard Boyatzis, and Annie McKee. *Primal Leadership: Unleashing the Power of Emotional Intelligence.* Harvard Business Review, 2013.

Goodwin, Doris Kearns. *Leadership in Turbulent Times.* Simon & Schuster, 2019.

Harvard Business School. "Virtual Books@Baker with Michael Beer on his book 'Fit to Compete.'" 2021, https://www.youtube.com/watch?v=3rfbqbZKwyg.

Insight Management Academy. "What Does Effective Insight Leadership Look Like?" https://www.insight-management.org/5-min-insight/what-does-effective-insight-leadership-look.

Lencioni, Patrick. *The Five Dysfunctions of a Team: A Leadership Fable.* Random House, audiobook, 2002.

McKenzie, Vashti M. *Not Without a Struggle: Leadership for African American Women in Ministry.* rev. ed. Pigrim Press, 2011.

Marquet, David. *Turn the Ship Around!: A True Story of Turning Followers into Leaders.* Portfolio, 2013.

Maxwell, John C. *The 21 Irrefutable Laws of Leadership: Follow Them and People Will Follow You.* HarperCollins, 2007.

Murphy, Joseph. *Essential Lessons for School Leaders: Tips for Courage, Finding Solutions, and Reaching Your Goals.* Corwin, 2011.

Murphy, Joseph F., and Karen Seashore Louis. *Positive School Leadership: Building Capacity and Strengthening Relationships.* Teacher College Press, 2018.

Pink, Daniel H. *Drive: The Surprising Truth About What Motivates Us.* Penguin, audiobook, 2009.

Pink, Daniel. "Purpose—Why We Do What We Do," 2013, https://www.youtube.com/watch?v=_p4esMj2EC8.

Rubenstein, David M. *How to Lead: Wisdom from the World's Greatest CEOs, Founders, and Game Changers.* Simon & Schuster, 2019.

Sinek, Simon. *Leaders Eat Last: Why Some Teams Pull Together and Others Don't*. Penguin, Audiobook, 2020.

Sinek, Simon. *Start with Why: How Great Leaders Inspire Everyone to Take Action*. Penguin, audiobook, 2017.

StackExchange. "What Is the Origin of the Phrase 'A Mountain I'm Willing to Die On'?" 2014. https://english.stackexchange.com/questions/162813/what-is-the-origin-of-the-phrase-a-mountain-im-willing-to-die-on.

Tulsiani, Ravinder. *Your Leadership Edge: Mastering Management Skills for Today's Workforce*. self-published, 2014.

www.ingramcontent.com/pod-product-compliance
Lightning Source LLC
Chambersburg PA
CBHW062225080426
42734CB00010B/2031